we★are★all★americans

We Are All Americans
The American Civil War Retold

by Richard A. Radoccia

ISBN-13: 978-1546767213

ISBN-10: 1546767215

Contents

Preface i

Prologue – The 1850's 1

Chapter 1 – The Election of 1860 5

Chapter 2 – Secession 11

Chapter 3 – Sumter 18

Chapter 4 – It's War 27

Chapter 5 – Union Spring 33

Chapter 6 – Enter Mr. Lee 39

Chapter 7 – The Prayer of Twenty Millions 46

Chapter 8 – Antietam 50

Chapter 9 – The Proclamation 55

Chapter 10 – The Mid-Terms 59

Chapter 11 – Carousel of Generals 63

Chapter 12 – Emancipation Changes Everything 71

Chapter 13 – Confederate Fortunes Rise 77

Chapter 14 – Races East and West 86

Chapter 15 – Joy and Despair 93

Chapter 16 – Abolition or Union 102

Chapter 17 – Grant Comes East 107

Chapter 18 – Lincoln under Pressure 118

Chapter 19 – War is Cruelty 122

Chapter 20 – A Second Term 127

Chapter 21 – Beginning of the End 131

Chapter 22 – With Malice toward None 139

Chapter 23 – Appomattox 145

Chapter 24 – Eulogy 158

Epilogue 161

Image Credits 164

NOTICE

The following is a recreation of an important historical event. In order to maintain authenticity and remain true to the historical record, there has been no editing of the actual written or spoken words.

The reader may find some language to be offensive and some photographs to be unsettling.

Discretion is advised.

Preface

Robert Penn Warren called the Civil War the "American oracle". It changed the country's destiny. It was the great pivot upon which the path of the American story forever turned.

One hundred and fifty plus years later, in an age where history is any news older than 24 hours, it is easy to think of the American Civil War as ancient history – or to not even think of it at all. Yet, for all the progress in race relations that has been made in the U.S. since then, it is unfortunately evident that bigotry and hatred of "those not like me" is still extant in the American fabric.

America elected its first black president in 2008 yet the resulting resentment fueled a commitment by political opposition leaders to destroy his presidency, even at the risk of harming the country and its citizenry. Political representatives of the "Party of Lincoln" unabashedly passed legislation specifically designed to prevent blacks and other minorities from voting. Ironically, Abraham Lincoln was assassinated for supporting enfranchisement for blacks.

The American Civil War was a time of extraordinary sacrifice. It was a time of genuine exceptionalism, when white men from essentially all walks of life sacrificed home, family and existence for the principle of human equality.

On April 9, 1865, Confederate General Robert E. Lee surrendered his Army of Northern Virginia to Union General Ulysses S. Grant at the McLean family home in Appomattox. Lt. Colonel Ely S. Parker, a Seneca Indian who became one of General Grant's closest friends and advisors, made the formal ink copy of the terms of surrender. Seeing that Parker was an American Indian, General Lee remarked to Parker, "I am glad to see one real American here." Parker replied, "Today, we are all Americans."

* * * * *

We hold these Truths to be self-evident, that all Men are created equal, that they are endowed by their Creator with certain unalienable Rights, that among these are Life, Liberty and the pursuit of Happiness.

The Declaration of Independence is America's cross to bear. And it is a heavy one at that.

Even the very men who penned the Declaration, which inspired the defeat of the world's most formidable army by a bunch of farmers, could not live up to its spirit when it came time to draft the U.S. Constitution eleven years later.

At the time of the Constitutional Convention, there were about half a million slaves in the United States, mostly in the five southernmost states, where they comprised 40% of the population. Hotly debated at the Convention was the issue of whether to include slaves in the calculation to determine state representation in Congress.

As expected, delegates from southern states argued that slaves should be considered "persons" to determine representation, but as "property" if the new government were to levy taxes on the basis of population. Northern state delegates, where slavery was uncommon, argued that slaves should be included in taxation, but, since they could not vote, should not be included in determining representation.

Americans today know this as the "taxation v. representation" debate.

The final compromise — to count "all other persons" as three-fifths of their actual numbers — reduced the representation of the slave states relative to original proposals, but improved their representation in relation to free-states. An inducement for slave states to accept the Compromise was its tie to taxation in the same ratio, so that the burden of taxation on slave states was also reduced.

The Three-Fifths Compromise gave slave states a disproportionate influence in the new central government, namely the presidency, through the Electoral College, the speakership of the House, and the Supreme Court.

This was not meaningless. Historian Garry Wills proposed that without the additional slave state votes, Thomas Jefferson would have lost the presidential election of 1800, Missouri would have been admitted as a free state, Andrew Jackson's Indian Removal Act would never have passed in Congress, and the Wilmot Proviso, which banned slavery in territories won from Mexico, would have passed.

The other key provision was Article IV, Section 2, "No person held to Service or Labour in one State" "escaping into another," "shall be discharged from such Service or Labour, but shall be delivered up on Claim of the Party to whom such Service or Labour may be due."

South Carolina delegates submitted this clause to the Constitutional Convention. Northern delegates objected, stating it would require that state governments enforce slavery at taxpayers' expense. Notwithstanding the objection, the clause was quietly reinstated and adopted by the Convention without objection.

Thomas Jefferson described the justification best when he said, "as it is, we have the wolf by the ear, and we can neither hold him nor safely let him go. Justice is in one scale, and self-preservation in the other."

In short, despite the lofty idealism of the Declaration, the United States was born under pragmatism leading to compromise, with the trade bait being slavery.

Even the strident abolitionist Benjamin Franklin waited until the Constitution was ratified to voice his opposition to slavery. His last public act was to petition Congress on behalf of the Pennsylvania Abolitionist Society to abolish slavery and end the slave trade. The petition, signed on February 3, 1790, asked the first Congress, then meeting in New York City, to "devise means for removing the Inconsistency from the Character of the American People," and to "promote mercy and justice toward this distressed Race."

Franklin's "Inconsistency" set the stage for civil war.

* * * * *

By virtue of the Three-Fifths Clause in the Constitution, southern or slaveholding states, despite being less populous, controlled the national government for much of the period between 1787 and 1860. In effect, the minority ruled the majority.

With that political power and the use of slave labor, in particular to the growing of cotton, the economy of the antebellum South grew rapidly. Between 1840 and 1860, per capita income in the South outpaced the rest of the nation. In 1860, the state with the highest per capita income was Mississippi. It took Italy almost 80 years – until the eve of World War II – to achieve the same level of per capita income.

Mid-century, the economic system of slavery was stronger than ever. Slave owners relished the opportunity to take this business model to California and Western Territories, Cuba and Latin America.

Much of the North did not necessarily stand in their way. Some of the country's wealthiest companies and families made their fortunes either directly or indirectly through slavery. With much of the South's cotton and sugar financed and traded by New York City merchants, the City actually contemplated joining the secession movement after South Carolina made the first move.

What did stand in their way was a growing social consciousness – abolitionism – fermented on the strength of its righteousness and the will power of many indomitable, eloquent and charismatic leaders. In time, the moral opposition to slavery made its way into politics and Free State legislation that increasingly widened the social, economic and political divide between the sections.

On June 16, 1858, Abraham Lincoln gave a speech upon being selected as the new Republican Party's candidate for the U.S. Senate against the Democratic candidate, Stephen A. Douglas. Lincoln's words apparently were too "candid" for the public to hear and often cited as the main reason he lost to Douglas.

> *A house divided against itself cannot stand. I believe this government cannot endure, permanently half slave and half free. I do not expect the Union to be dissolved – I do not expect the house to fall -- but I do expect it will cease to be divided. It will become all one thing or all the other.*

Without stating so directly, Lincoln predicted war. The future was binary – the United States, or the Union, would be all free or cease to exist. There was no third option of "half slave and half free".

Southerners, however, were in no frame of mind to change their way of life or abolish their peculiar institution. Increasingly, Northerners were not willing to simply let slavery be.

This conflict of interests and wills overwhelmed further compromise with the election of Lincoln in 1860. The minority was threatened when the majority took control of the national government, unquestionably fearing it would seek to first contain and then abolish slavery. In response, the minority seceded and formed a "new national government" that would preserve slavery.

The South's political objective to become an independent state in order to protect slavery was countered by the North's political objective to preserve the single democratic state memorialized in George Washington's first inaugural when he referred to the "indissoluble union".

* * * * *

The story is presented in chronological order, beginning with the election of 1860, by three "contemporary" reporters speaking from a newsroom that is all too familiar today. Their narration is intermixed with the actual words of three of the most important "historical" characters: Jefferson Davis, Frederick Douglass and Abraham Lincoln.

Tying the narrative to its true chronological order is, I believe, essential to gaining an appreciation of the event. Political and battlefield happenings brought incredible highs and lows to public sentiment on both sides.

I do not think it is possible to "grasp" the story of the Civil War without this sense of "being there" because the homeland sentiment, in return, affected so much of what could be achieved back in the political and battlefield arenas.

* * * * *

Lastly, I end this introduction of why I felt compelled to undertake this project with a few words from Robert E. Lee, who said it better than I could.

> "The March of Providence is so slow, and our desires so impatient, the work of progress is so immense, and our means to aid it so feeble, the life of humanity is so long, and that of the individual so brief, that we often see only the ebb of the advancing wave, and we are thus discouraged.
>
> It is history that teaches us to hope."

Prologue – The 1850's

The 1850's began with the passage of the Fugitive Slave Act as part of the Compromise of 1850 that sought to quell sectional discord and keep the Union intact. The Act required officials and citizens of Free states to cooperate in the return of escaped slaves. For those Americans at the silent center of the slavery question, it forced them to support slavery in their own, supposedly 'free' backyards.

The Act was so emotionally contentious that it helped the Abolitionist movement gain considerable traction among a wide swath of Northerners. Taking a cue from Henry David Thoreau's *Civil Disobedience* (1849), many Free states enacted 'personal liberty laws' or other devices to effectively nullify this Federal law. The conscience of the North began to move towards Abolitionism.

In 1852, Harriet Beecher Stowe's *Uncle Tom's Cabin* gave the movement a shove by personifying the cruelty of slavery. It sold 300,000 copies in its first year, the equivalent of what would be 5 million today. The United States would never be the same.

Frederick Douglass was an escaped slave. With a gift of oratory and literary eloquence, Douglass became an international celebrity speaking in Ireland and Britain. He returned to the US in 1847 to save his brethren in bondage through speeches and anti-slavery publications.

In 1852, the Ladies of the Rochester Anti-Slavery Sewing Society invited Douglass to deliver an Independence Day address. Called the "What to the slave is the 4th of July?" speech, it is to this day regarded as one of the great speeches in American history.

Fellow Citizens, I am not wanting in respect for the fathers of this republic. The signers of the Declaration of Independence were brave men. They were great men. I will unite with you to honor their memory.

Your fathers staked their lives, their fortunes, and their sacred honor, on the cause of their country. Their solid manhood stands out the more as we contrast it with these degenerate times.

I do not hesitate to declare with all my soul that the character and conduct of this nation never looked blacker to me than on this Fourth of July!

Fellow citizens, pardon me, and allow me to ask, why am I called upon to speak here today? What have I or those I represent to do with your national independence? Are the great principles of political freedom and of natural justice, embodied in that Declaration of Independence, extended to us?

The blessings in which you this day rejoice are not enjoyed in common. The rich inheritance of justice, liberty, prosperity, and independence bequeathed by your fathers is shared by you, not by me. The sunlight that brought life and healing to you has brought stripes and death to me. This Fourth of July is yours, not mine.

You declare before the world, and are understood by the world to declare that you "hold these truths to be self-evident, that all men are created equal; and are endowed by their Creator with certain in alienable rights; and that among these are, life, liberty, and the pursuit of happiness; and yet, you hold securely, in a bondage which, according to your own Thomas Jefferson, "is worse than ages of that which your fathers rose in rebellion to oppose," a seventh part of the inhabitants of your country.

Whether we turn to the declarations of the past, or to the professions of the present, the conduct of the nation seems equally hideous and revolting.

What, to the American slave, is your Fourth of July? I answer: a day that reveals to him, more than all other days in the year, the gross injustice and cruelty to which he is the constant victim.

To him, your celebration is a sham; your boasted liberty, an unholy license; your shouts of liberty and equality, hollow mockery; your prayers and hymns, your sermons and thanksgivings, are, to Him, mere bombast, fraud, deception, impiety, and hypocrisy - a thin veil to cover up crimes which would disgrace a nation of savages.

For it is not light that is needed, but fire; it is not the gentle shower, but thunder. We need the storm, the whirlwind, and the earthquake. The hypocrisy of the nation must be exposed; and its crimes against God and man must be denounced.

At the end of the decade, on the night of October 16, 1859, a zealous abolitionist named John Brown organized a raid on the Federal arsenal at Harper's Ferry, Virginia in an attempt to arm slaves and spark an uprising against slaveholders. Word of the raid, however, reached townspeople before it reached slaves.

The raid was a complete failure. A company of U.S. Marines, led by Colonel Robert E. Lee and Lieutenant J. E. B. Stuart, arrived on the 18th. Brown was wounded and captured while ten of his men, including two of his sons, were killed.

Despite pleas from the likes of Henry David Thoreau and Northern abolitionists, Brown was tried by the state of Virginia for treason and murder and found guilty on November 2. Brown was tried and executed – as a terrorist in the South, as a martyr in the North.

John Brown's death did more to end slavery than he could have accomplished in life.

Before he was hanged on December 2, 1859, he handed a guard a note that read, "I, John Brown, am now quite certain that the crimes of this guilty land will never be purged away but with blood."

It was a prophetic statement.

When Confederate General Robert E. Lee surrendered the Army of Northern Virginia to U.S. Lt. Gen. Ulysses S. Grant on April 9, 1865, the American Civil War finally ended. The blood spent to "purge the land of its guilt" was nothing short of colossal.

To this day, total casualties of the American Civil War still exceed the combined total of all other wars fought by the United States.

Chapter 1 – The Election of 1860

*A*braham Lincoln gains national fame debating Stephen A. Douglas for the Illinois Senate seat in 1858. The "Little Giant", as Douglas was nicknamed, again faces Lincoln in the presidential election of 1860. Many of the issues previously debated by the two men are factors in the general election.

Despite frequently declaring that he is not an abolitionist, Lincoln states he is morally opposed to slavery and that it should not be allowed to expand into Federal territories. That is enough for Southerners to intensify their threats to break up the Union if Lincoln were to be elected.

As for Stephen Douglas, he is caught in the unfavorable position of being a Southern sympathizer just as events, including the John Brown saga, fuel the momentum of abolitionism across the North. Attempting to appeal to both sides, Douglas loses his Southern support and the Democratic Party splits. That split gives the opening for Lincoln and the Republican Party to take control of the Federal government.

November 7, 1860

ANDERSON: Good evening and welcome to American News Network's special coverage of Election Night 1860. Carter Anderson reporting.

This is truly an historic night as Northerners turned out in near all-out fashion to elect Abraham Lincoln the next and 16th President of the United States. Overall, 82% of eligible voters cast a ballot.

Mr. Lincoln, running on a platform to limit the extension of slavery in the Territories but not in those states where

slavery already exists, defeated his old foe, Sen. Stephen A. Douglas.

Mr. Lincoln, who garnered national fame while debating Mr. Douglas for the Illinois Senate office in 1858, won the electoral votes of every Free State except New Jersey, which went to Mr. Douglas.

However, there is another side to this story, one that portends some trying days ahead for the country. For that report, we go to Jackie Chase at Republican Campaign Headquarters in New York.

CHASE: Thank you, Carter. You are indeed correct – this election may be a defining moment in the American democratic experiment. If we look at the results, we can see just how divided the country is.

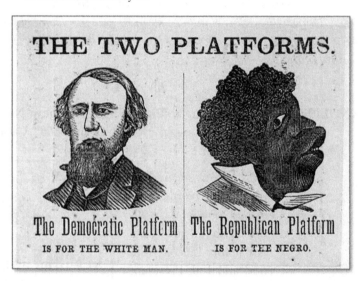

THE TWO PLATFORMS.

The Democratic Platform | The Republican Platform

IS FOR THE WHITE MAN. | IS FOR THE NEGRO.

While Mr. Lincoln swept the North, he won only 40% of the popular vote. In Missouri, Kentucky, Maryland and Delaware, Mr. Lincoln won only two of 996 counties.

The Northern Democratic nominee, Senator Douglas, won 30% of the popular vote, leaving him just 480,000 votes shy of Mr. Lincoln. Mr. Douglas, known as the Little Giant, ran

on a platform that appealed to those who fear a Republican victory will bring an end to the Union.

Many of the Republican campaign workers I spoke to tonight said that Mr. Lincoln is like them – a common man with a humble beginning who taught himself to read, eventually becoming a lawyer who argued before the Supreme Court. From the time he was a Congressman, Mr. Lincoln has remained steadfast in his opposition to the expansion of slavery and its moral failings. They trust he will not let them down and capitulate to the power of slave owners as prior presidents have done before.

ANDERSON: Thank you, Jackie. It does appear that Northerners declared with their votes that the matter of slavery needs to be settled now.

For the past several decades, Southern leaders have threatened secession if they did not get their way. These threats became more thunderous over the past few months as early voting favored Mr. Lincoln.

Will we now see Southerners turn those threats into action?

For more on Southern reaction to Lincoln's election, let's go to Danielle Burke at Southern Democratic Headquarters in Richmond, Virginia.

BURKE: Carter, the reaction here to the election results can best be described as "outraged" and "defiant."

THE UNITED STATES—A BLACK BUSINESS

Southern leaders say that Lincoln as president means tyranny in the South.

Though Mr. Lincoln has stated publicly he is not an abolitionist, Southerners apparently do not trust him.

The Richmond Examiner's lead story says, "The party founded on the single sentiment of hatred of African slavery is now the controlling power."

And the *New Orleans Delta* declared, "No one should be deluded that the Black Republican Party is a moderate party. In fact it is essentially a revolutionary party."

ANDERSON: Danielle, the Republicans have gained power through lawful, constitutional means. If slave states secede, wouldn't they be the revolutionaries?

BURKE: That is a good question. Throughout history, revolutions, including our own, typically attempt to change the status quo. Should any slave state actually secede, it will be to protect the status quo.

LITTLE BO-PEEP AND HER FOOLISH SHEEP.

ANDERSON: Along those lines, we just got word that the governor of South Carolina has called the state legislature into special session tomorrow to consider secession.

Mr. Lincoln does not take the oath of office until March 4, 1861, four months from now. That seems like an eternity with how quickly events are unfolding.

* * * * *

DOUGLASS: The deed is now done and a new order of events connected with the great question of slavery, is now fairly opening upon the country, the end whereof the most sagacious and far-sighted are unable to see and declare.

It was a contest between sections, North and South, as to what shall be the principles and policy of the national Government in respect to the slave system of the fifteen Southern States.

For fifty years, the country has taken the law from the lips of an exacting, haughty and imperious slave oligarchy. The masters of slaves have been masters of the Republic. Their authority was almost undisputed, and their power irresistible.

They were the President makers of the Republic, and no aspirant dared to hope for success against their frown.

Lincoln's election has vitiated their authority and broken their power. It has taught the North its strength, and shown the South its weakness. More important still, it has demonstrated the possibility of electing, if not an Abolitionist, at least an anti-slavery reputation to the Presidency of the United States.

The years are few since it was thought possible that the Northern people could be wrought up to the exercise of such startling courage.

Hitherto the threat of disunion has been as potent over the politicians of the North, as the cat-o'-nine-tails is over the backs of the slaves. Mr. Lincoln's election breaks this enchantment, dispels this terrible nightmare, and awakens the nation to the consciousness of new powers, and the possibility of a higher destiny than the perpetual bondage to an ignoble fear.

Chapter 2 – Secession

*O*n May 1, 1833, President Andrew Jackson wrote presciently, "the tariff was only a pretext, and disunion and southern confederacy the real object. The next pretext will be the negro, or slavery question."

The issue of states' rights v. Federal powers dominates the next two decades. Ironically, in the years leading up to the Civil War, it is the Northerners who use the argument of states' rights to nullify the execution of the Fugitive Slave Act while Southerners seek to expand the power of the Federal government to protect and expand slavery. The roles reverse with the election of Abraham Lincoln. After decades of threatening to leave the union, Southerners, led by South Carolina, act.

December 3, 1860

ANDERSON:

In his final message to Congress today, President Buchanan surprised many Southerners by stating that the framers "never intended to implant in its bosom the seeds of its own destruction, nor were they guilty of the absurdity of providing for its own dissolution."

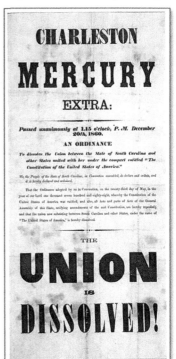

CHASE:

Carter, the *Cincinnati Daily Commercial* echoed the President's message with an editorial that equates secession with anarchy. "If any minority has the right to break up the Government at pleasure, because they have not had their way, there is an end of all government."

December 18, 1860

ANDERSON:

With tensions escalating and rhetoric becoming increasingly belligerent, the House of Representatives and the Senate today voted down a proposal prepared by Kentucky Senator John J. Crittenden that would amend the Constitution to make slavery permanent in the slave states, prohibit interference of Fugitive Slave Laws, and allow for the expansion of slavery to new western states.

Republicans refused to support the measure, apparently after learning of Mr. Lincoln's guidance.

LINCOLN:

The tug has to come, and better now, than any time hereafter. The proposal would lose us everything we gained by the election and put us again on the high road to a slave empire.

We have just carried an election on principles fairly stated to the people. Now we are told in advance, the government shall be broken up unless we surrender to those we have beaten.

If we surrender, it is the end of us.

DAVIS: The time for compromise has now passed. The South is determined to maintain her position and make all who oppose her smell Southern powder and feel Southern steel.

December 20, 1860

BURKE: This is Danielle Burke reporting from Charleston, South Carolina, where a celebration is underway following a unanimous vote by the delegates to the Convention of the People of South Carolina to secede from the Unites States. Eight military companies paraded down Main Street under a shower of rockets and fireworks while the band played the "Marseillaise".

Governor Pickens was serenaded at the Mills House by a buoyant crowd. He promised to reopen the African slave trade, declare white men the ruling race and punish "summarily and severely, if not with death" any person caught espousing abolitionist views.

December 26, 1860

CHASE: This is Jackie Chase from Washington DC. At precisely the noon hour today in Charleston Harbor, the Stars and Stripes was raised on a flagpole at Fort Sumter by the Federal garrison that left Fort Moultrie under the dark of night under the leadership of Major Robert Anderson.

Robert Anderson, born in Kentucky and raised in Virginia, is the son of a Revolutionary War soldier who actually defended the same fort more than 80 years ago.

The Major led his men from a certain defeat at Fort Moultrie to a much safer and stronger Fort Sumter completely surprising the South Carolina militia that had Moultrie surrounded.

The actions by Major Anderson and his men have engendered pride across the North.

January 11, 1861

ANDERSON:

A unified Southern Confederacy is almost a reality this evening. Today, Alabama followed Florida yesterday and Mississippi on the 9th to become the

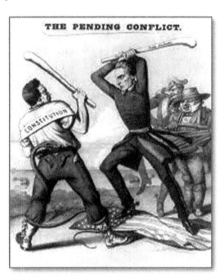

second, third and fourth states to declare independence from the Union.

Alabama's Ordinance of Secession was passed in Montgomery to the accompaniment of bells, cannon fire and whoops from the large crowd gathered outside the convention hall.

January 19, 1861

BURKE:

Georgia joined its Southern brethren today to become the fifth state to secede from the Union.

January 26, 1861

CHASE: The Confederacy of the United States is quickly taking shape as word has just arrived in Washington that Louisiana voted become the sixth state to secede.

February 1, 1861

ANDERSON: Over the objections of Governor Sam Houston, who made clear his allegiance to the Union, the Texas legislature voted to secede. The result was never in question as 70 votes were cast in favor of secession before a single nay was cast.

February 11, 1861

CHASE: One day before his fifty-second birthday, President-Elect Abraham Lincoln boarded a train in Springfield, Illinois to travel to Washington, DC today. Mr. Lincoln shook hands with well-wishers in the waiting room at the train station and then walked on to the rear platform of the passenger car. When he removed his hat, the rain trickled down his face, which quivered with emotion.

LINCOLN: I now leave, not knowing when, or whether ever, I may return, with a task before me greater than that which rests upon Washington. Without the assistance of that Divine Being who ever attended him, I cannot succeed. With that assistance, I cannot fail. Trusting in Him who can go with me and remain with you and be everywhere for good, let us confidently hope that all will yet be well. To His care commending you, as I hope, in your prayers, you will commend me. I bid you an affectionate farewell.

February 14, 1861

BURKE:

The Confederacy has its first leader this morning, following the election of Jefferson Davis as President by a unanimous vote at the national convention in Montgomery yesterday.

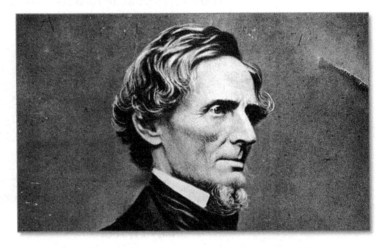

DAVIS:

I enter upon the duties of the office to which I have been chosen with the hope that the beginning of our career as a Confederacy may not be obstructed by hostile opposition to our enjoyment of the separate existence and independence which we have asserted, and, with the blessing of Providence, intend to maintain.

Our present condition, achieved in a manner unprecedented in the history of nations, illustrates the American idea that governments rest upon the consent of the governed, and that it is the right of the people to alter or abolish governments whenever they become destructive of the ends for which they were established.

If a just perception of mutual interest shall permit us peaceably to pursue our separate political career, my most earnest desire will have been fulfilled.

But, if this be denied to us, and the integrity of our territory and jurisdiction be assailed, it will but remain for us, with firm resolve, to appeal to arms and invoke the blessings of Providence on a just cause.

Chapter 3 – Sumter

*L*incoln is sworn into office of a country that is rapidly coming apart. Though he extends an olive branch to Southern leaders, he refuses to concede Fort Sumter. South Carolina militia bombards the fort with a U.S. garrison inside. In response, Lincoln raises an army to protect Federal property. As a result, Virginia, the most populous Southern state, secedes. Three other states immediately follow to join the Confederacy. Lincoln offers the command of the U.S. Army to U.S. Colonel Robert E. Lee. He replies he could not fight against his homeland of Virginia.

March 4, 1861

CHASE: Today, Abraham Lincoln was sworn in as the 16th president of the United States of America.

LINCOLN: Here is the cause of the trouble. It is slavery, the sum of all villainies, on the one hand, and all the silent but mighty forces of nature on the other. Here is and must ever remain the irrepressible conflict, until slavery is abolished, or human nature, with all its divine attributes, is changed and made to reflect the image of hell instead of heaven.

OUR NATIONAL BIRD AS IT APPEARED WHEN HANDED TO JAMES BUCHANAN. MARCH 4.1857.

THE IDENTICAL BIRD AS IT APPEARED .A .D. 1861.

It is seventy-two years since the first inauguration of a President under our National Constitution. During that period, fifteen different and greatly distinguished citizens have in succession administered the executive branch of the Government. They have conducted it through many perils, and generally with great success.

Yet, with all this scope of precedent, I now enter upon the same task for the brief constitutional term of four years under great and peculiar difficulty. A disruption of the Federal Union, heretofore only menaced, is now formidably attempted.

Plainly, the central idea of secession is the essence of anarchy. A majority held in restraint by constitutional checks and limitations, and always changing easily with deliberate changes of popular opinions and sentiments, is the only true sovereign of a free people.

Unanimity is impossible. The rule of a minority, as a permanent arrangement, is wholly inadmissible; so that, rejecting the majority principle, anarchy or despotism in some form is all that is left.

In your hands, my dissatisfied fellow-countrymen, and not in mine, is the momentous issue of civil war. The Government will not assail you. You can have no conflict without being yourselves the aggressors. You have no oath registered in heaven to destroy the Government, while I shall have the most solemn one to "preserve, protect, and defend it."

We are not enemies, but friends. We must not be enemies. Though passion may have strained it must not break our bonds of affection. The mystic chords of memory, stretching from every battlefield and patriot grave to every living heart and hearthstone all over this broad land will yet swell the chorus of the Union, when again touched, as surely they will be, by the better angels of our nature.

April 12, 1861

ANDERSON:

At 4:30AM this morning, Confederate batteries stationed around Charleston Harbor opened fire on Fort Sumter and the Federal garrison under the command of Major Robert Anderson. Three Navy vessels sent by President Lincoln to bring food to the men were steaming towards the mouth of the harbor when the shots rang out.

April 14, 1861

BURKE:

Today, the American stars and stripes came down and the Confederate stars and bars rose over Fort Sumter as the Federal garrison surrendered.

LINCOLN:

They attacked Sumter – it fell, and thus, did more service than it otherwise could.

DAVIS:

Fort Sumter is ours, and nobody is hurt. With mortar, Paixhan and petard we tender 'OLD ABE' our Beau-regards.

April 15, 1861

CHASE:

In the aftermath of the surrender of Fort Sumter, President Lincoln today issued a proclamation to call-up 75,000 troops for a 90-day period. Almost immediately, the White House was besieged by telegrams expressing their support, including from Stephen Douglas, who ran against him in the election.

Indiana was asked to supply six regiments, the governor offered twelve. Ohio offered twenty. Governor Andrew of Massachusetts wired that two regiments are already on their way to Washington.

However, some in the military believe many more will be

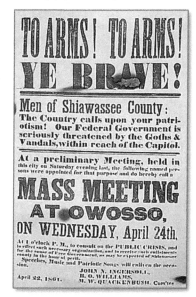

needed. U.S. Colonel William T. Sherman said, "Why, you might as well attempt to put out the flames of a burning house with a squirt-gun."

April 17, 1861

BURKE:

In an emergency session today, the Virginia Convention voted to secede from the United States. This meeting was held in response to President Lincoln's call for troops. Participants said, "Virginians can never fight our Southern brethren."

April 20, 1861

ANDERSON:

With the statue of the Father of our Country standing tall above a crowd of over 200,000 in New York's Union Square today, Major Robert Anderson arrived carrying the 33-star flag that had flown above Fort Sumter. The multitude gathered in support of the Union cause following the capture of the South Carolina fort and the President's call for militia to quell the insurrection. The president of the New York Chamber of Commerce declared, "We are either for the country or for its enemies."

April 29, 1861

DAVIS:

African slavery, as it exists in the United States, is a moral, a social, and a political blessing.

Under the mild and genial climate of the Southern States and the increasing care and attention for the wellbeing and comfort of the laboring class, dictated alike by interest and humanity, the African slaves have augmented in number from about 600,000, at the date of the adoption of the constitutional compact, to upward of 4,000,000.

In moral and social condition, they have been elevated from brutal savages into docile, intelligent, and civilized agricultural laborers, and supplied not only with bodily comforts but also with careful religious instruction.

Under the supervision of a superior race, their labor has been so directed as not only to allow a gradual and marked amelioration of their own condition, but to convert hundreds of thousands of square miles of the wilderness into cultivated lands covered with a prosperous people; towns and cities have sprung into existence, rapidly increasing in wealth and population under the social system of the South.

We feel that our cause is just and holy; we protest solemnly in the face of mankind that we desire peace at any sacrifice save that of honor and independence; we seek no conquest, no aggrandizement, no concession of any kind from the States with which we were lately confederated; all we ask is to be let alone; that those who never held power over us shall not now attempt our subjugation by arms.

This we will, this we must, resist to the direst extremity.

May 3, 1861

CHASE: Union General-in-Chief Winfield Scott presented his plan to defeat the Confederacy to President Lincoln today.

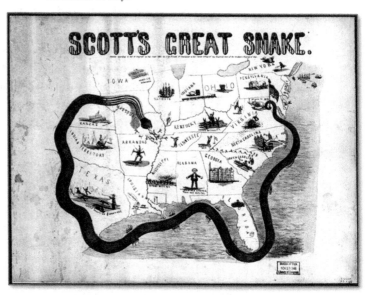

The plan calls for an effective "blockade" of Southern ports, a strong thrust down the Mississippi Valley with a large force, and the establishment of a line of strong Federal positions to isolate the disorganized Confederate nation "to squeeze the South to military death." Scott proposed that 60,000 troops move down the Mississippi with gunboats until they secure the river from Cairo, Ill., to the Gulf, which, in concert with an effective blockade, would seal off the South.

May 6, 1861

BURKE: Arkansas lawmakers voted 65-5 today, becoming the ninth Southern state to join the Confederate States of America.

May 20, 1861

ANDERSON: The state of North Carolina voted today to secede from the American Union. This date was chosen to celebrate the anniversary of the Mecklenburg Declaration of Independence of 1775.

June 8, 1861

BURKE:

The state of Tennessee voted to secede today in a very close referendum. Eastern Tennessee, firmly supportive of the Union, voted "against" separation while the western third of the state voted "for" with equal weight. In February, middle Tennessee barely kept the state in the fold with a 51% vote "against." With emotions running high across the South, the middle overwhelmingly voted to secede and join the Confederacy as its eleventh state.

* * * * *

DOUGLASS:

Slavery is the disease, and its abolition in every part of the land is essential to the future quiet and security of the country.

It is a matter of life and death. Slavery must be all in the Union, or it can be nothing. This is fully understood by the slaveholders of the cotton States and hence they can accept no compromise, no concession, no settlement that does not exalt slavery above every other interest in the country.

If there is not wisdom and virtue enough in the land to rid the country of slavery, then the next best thing is to let the South go to her own place, and be made to drink the wine cup of wrath and fire, which her long career of cruelty, barbarism and blood shall call down upon her guilty head.

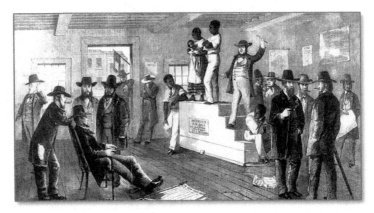

The contest must now be decided, and decided forever, which of the two, Freedom or Slavery, shall give law to this Republic. Let the conflict come.

For this consummation we have watched and wished with fear and trembling. God be praised that it has come at last.

Chapter 4 – It's War

*M*ost do not anticipate a long war ahead. Southerners cried wolf so often that Northerners see the secessions as another tactic to get the more populous North to acquiesce to its demands.

This time, however, the South is not bluffing. In electing Jefferson Davis as its President, the Confederacy goes all-in – independence or extermination is how Davis would later describe their purpose.

After the Confederates rout the raw Federal soldiers at Bull Run, Lincoln follows suit and 'escalates' the war with substantial call-ups and puts the Union war production effort into high gear.

July 4, 1861

LINCOLN: I now recommend that you give the legal means for making this contest a short and a decisive one; that you place at the control of the Government for the work at least 400,000 men and $400,000,000.

It is now for us to demonstrate to the world that those who can fairly carry an election can also suppress a rebellion; that ballots are the rightful and peaceful successors of bullets, and that when ballots have fairly and constitutionally decided there can be no successful appeal back to bullets; that there can be no successful appeal except to ballots themselves at succeeding elections. Such will be a great lesson of peace, teaching men that, what they cannot take by an election, neither can they take it by a war; teaching all the folly of being the beginners of a war.

DAVIS:

Secession belongs to a different class of remedies. It is to be justified upon the basis that the States are sovereign.

We have heard proclaimed the theory that all men are created free and equal; and the sacred Declaration of Independence has been invoked to maintain the position of the equality of the races.

These were the great principles they announced; these were the purposes for which they made their declaration; these were the ends to which their enunciation was directed. They have no reference to the slave.

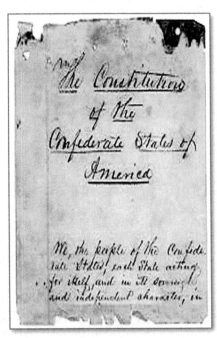

When our Constitution was formed, the same idea was rendered more palpable, for there we find provision made for that very class of persons as property; they were not put upon the footing of equality with white men--not even upon that of paupers and convicts; but, so far as representation was concerned, were discriminated against as a lower caste, only to be represented in the numerical proportion of three fifths.

We recur to the principles upon which our Government was founded; and when you deny them, and when you deny to us the right to withdraw from a Government which threatens to be destructive of our rights, we tread in the path of our fathers when we proclaim our independence and take the hazard.

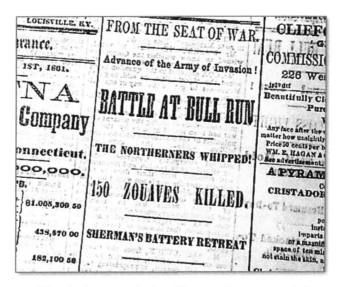

This is done not in hostility to others, not to injure any section of the country, not even for our own pecuniary benefit; but from the high and solemn motive of defending and protecting the rights we inherited, and which it is our sacred duty to transmit unshorn to our children.

July 21, 1861

CHASE: This is Jackie Chase reporting from Fairfax Court House where reporters, congressmen and civilians have gathered on this very hot and sultry morning to witness first-hand what appears to be a Union victory this morning as Federal soldiers crossed Bull Run and attacked the Confederate left flank. General Irvin McDowell headquarters reports that Southern regiments are fleeing to the rear.

BURKE:	This is Danielle Burke embedded with Confederate forces at Henry House Hill where a Virginia brigade under Colonel Thomas J. Jackson stopped the Union assault around noon. At 4PM, General Joseph Johnston sent in fresh troops who screamed in a way that pierced the heavens as they counterattacked, sending exhausted Union soldiers into retreat, dropping guns and packs along the way.
CHASE:	What looked like a victory has turned into a rout this afternoon as Union soldiers fleeing across Bull Run converged with panic-stricken onlookers. I spoke to one Congressman who said, "We called to them, tried to tell them there was no danger, called them to stop, implored them to stand. We called them cowards, threatened to shoot them, but all in vain; a cruel, crazy mad, hopeless panic possessed them."
BURKE:	Anxious for news of the battle, President Davis arrived on the scene on horseback this afternoon.

General Johnston returned from the front to declare victory. Soldiers are rejoicing. One observer said, "The victory secures our independence." Another said, "This hard fought battle virtually closes the war."

LINCOLN: The fat is in the fire now and we shall have to crow small until we can retrieve the disgrace somehow. The preparation for the war will be continued with increased vigor by the Government.

July 25, 1861

CHASE: President Abraham Lincoln signed a bill today authorizing the enlistment of 500,000 men to three-year deployments. This comes on the heels of a similar bill signed by the

President three days ago also calling for 500,000 men. Meanwhile, Mr. Lincoln has given command of this new Army of the Potomac to Major General George B. McClellan and instructed Union armies in the west to take the offensive.

August 8, 1861

BURKE: The Confederate Congress and President Davis called for 400,000 volunteers to serve for one or three years.

Chapter 5 – Union Spring

*U*nion *General Ulysses S. Grant gains Northern attention by capturing Confederate forts, cities and soldiers along the Mississippi Valley. However, the victories are achieved with an unexpectedly great loss of life and limb. For the first time, the war's human cost begins to concern the Northern populace.*

When "little Napoleon" General George McClellan got the Army of the Potomac within six miles of Richmond, combined with victories by western armies and the navy, Northern spirits and expectations of a short war soared.

February 16, 1862

ANDERSON: Following the President's order to go on the offensive and implement General Scott's "Anaconda Plan," Union forces in the Western Theater under General Ulysses S. Grant captured Fort Henry on the Tennessee River. They then surrounded Fort Donelson on the Cumberland River. Confederate General Simon Bolivar Buckner requested an armistice and terms of surrender from General Grant, who replied, "No terms except unconditional and immediate surrender can be accepted." Along with taking control

of the Cumberland River, Federal troops today

captured 12,000 Rebel soldiers, 48 artillery pieces and equipment.

CHASE: Carter, telegraph machines across the North immediately began tapping with this latest news. Cannons fired and church bells rang. Journalists christened the victorious Union general, "Unconditional Surrender" Grant. President Lincoln immediately promoted him to the rank of Major General.

February 22, 1862

BURKE: Anguish prevails across the south as news of the evacuation of Nashville and the capture of Roanoke Island follow the surrender of Forts Henry and Donelson. Confederate diplomat in London, James Mason, who is there seeking recognition and support from Great Britain, said, "The late reverses have had an unfortunate effect upon the minds of our friends here."

DAVIS: After a series of successes and victories, which covered our arms with glory, we have recently met with serious disasters. Although the contest is not ended, and the tide for the moment is against us, the final result in our favor is not doubtful.

It was, perhaps, in the ordination of Providence that we were to be taught the value of our liberties by the price which we pay for them.

April 7, 1862

ANDERSON: At Pittsburgh Landing, Tennessee, near Shiloh Church, a name that ironically means "Place of Peace," bloodshed has reached a new high where two days of fighting have left 24,000 men on both sides dead, dying or wounded. This death toll is greater than the totals of all battles to date.

Union General William Tecumseh Sherman described the aftermath as "piles of dead soldiers' mangled bodies, without heads and legs. The scenes on this field would cure anybody of war."

April 16, 1862

BURKE:

President Davis signed into law the first conscription law in American history, declaring all able-bodied white males between 18 and 35 liable to service for three years. The law immediately met with opposition from governors who see a national draft as a contradiction to the reasons states seceded. One North Carolina soldier said, "When we hear men comparing the despotism of the Confederacy with that of the Lincoln government, something must be wrong."

April 25, 1862

ANDERSON:

Today, the jewel of the Confederacy, the City of New Orleans, surrendered to Union Naval forces commanded by Admiral David G. Farragut. In addition to being the South's largest city, New Orleans is home to industry that produces ironclads, munitions and uniforms. Perhaps most importantly, the city controls access to the Mississippi River from the Gulf of Mexico.

Combined with advances down the River from the North, the Union is getting closer to the goal of the Anaconda Plan.

May 4, 1862

CHASE:

Carter, Union forces are also gaining ground in the Eastern Theater. We have just learned that Confederate forces have evacuated Yorktown, Virginia. General Joseph E. Johnston moved his forces back to Richmond after facing the Union in a standstill since April 5th.

Major General George B McClellan wired Secretary of War Edwin M. Stanton that he was on the move. "The enemy abandoned Yorktown last night and it is now in our possession. I have thrown all my cavalry in pursuit of the enemy. I shall push the enemy to the wall."

In the wake of these developments, public opinion in the North is riding high. The *New York Tribune* writes, "The cause of the Union now marches on in every section of the country. Every blow tells fearfully against the rebellion. The rebels are panic-stricken or despondent. It now requires no very far-reaching prophet to predict the end of the struggle."

WAR NEWS!

Victory!!

NEW ORLEANS TAKEN!

GREAT EXCITEMENT IN THE CITY.

DESTRUCTION OF COTTON AND STEAM BOATS.

Consternation of the Inhabitants.

BURKE:

The value of the Confederate dollar has fallen to a new

low. It now takes nearly three Confederate dollars to buy what one dollar bought at the beginning of last year.

June 21, 1862

ANDERSON:
The Union army and navy in the Western Theater now control most of the Mississippi River Valley from the North down to Memphis and from the Gulf of Mexico to New Orleans. Today, Union forces departed from Baton Rouge in vessels escorted by gunboats under Admiral Farragut, who declared, "The objective is Vicksburg, the Gibraltar of the Confederacy."

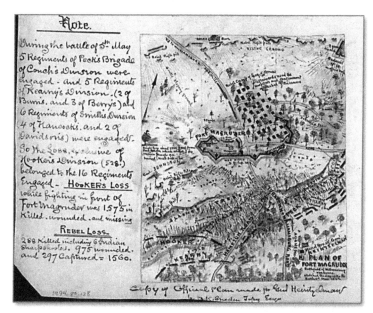

DAVIS:
Vicksburg is the nail head that holds the South's two halves together.

LINCOLN:
See what a lot of land these fellows hold, of which Vicksburg is the key! The war can never be brought to a close until that key is in our pocket. We can take all the northern ports of the Confederacy, and they can defy us from Vicksburg. As valuable as

New Orleans will be to us, Vicksburg will be more so.

Chapter 6 – Enter Mr. Lee

*W*hen *Confederate General Joseph Johnston is wounded defending the Virginia Peninsula against McClellan's advance, President Davis replaces him with Robert E. Lee. Confederate fortunes ascend quickly. Lee proves to be a superb field commander who uses his cavalry and daring to repeatedly defeat a much larger and better-equipped foe.*

July 2, 1862

ANDERSON: A stunning reversal of fortunes has occurred over the past seven days and through six major battles fought along the Virginia Peninsula. Confederate General Robert E. Lee drove the invading Union Army of the Potomac, commanded by Maj. Gen. George B. McClellan, away from Richmond and into a retreat.

General Lee assumed command of the Army of Northern Virginia only one month ago. For more on who is General Lee, let's go to Danielle Burke in Richmond.

BURKE: General Robert E. Lee hails from a prominent military family and background. His father was a

Revolutionary War officer and Lee himself was a top graduate and then Superintendent of the U.S. Military Academy at West Point.

He distinguished himself during the Mexican-American War and commanded the troops at Harpers Ferry who captured John Brown and his followers.

Lee was appointed Colonel of the First Regiment of Cavalry in March 1861 by the new President, Abraham Lincoln. Three weeks later, Colonel Lee was offered the rank of Major General in the expanding Army to fight the Southern States that had left the Union. When Virginia seceded, Lee chose Virginia and resigned from the Army on April 20.

Southern editorials immediately objected to this appointment, describing him as 'timid.' This may be partly due to Lee's outspoken objection to secession at the beginning of the war, denouncing it as "revolution" and a betrayal of the efforts of the founders. Lee stated, "I can anticipate no greater calamity for the country than a dissolution of the Union."

July 10, 1862

ANDERSON:

Over the past two weeks, both North and South demonstrated an extraordinary capacity to fight on despite persistent stress and exhaustion. Casualties have been very high for both armies.

After a successful start on the Peninsula that foretold an early end to the war, Northern morale has taken a body blow from McClellan's retreat. But, as we have seen throughout the conflict, President Lincoln seems to dig deeper after Union setbacks.

LINCOLN:

This war can no longer be fought with elder-stalk squirts, charged with rose water. This government cannot much longer play a game in which it stakes all, and its enemies stake nothing. Those enemies must understand that they cannot experiment for ten years trying to destroy the government, and, if they fail, still come back into the Union unhurt. It is time that they should begin to feel the presence of the war.

OMAHA CITY:

Friday,················July 4, 1862.

THE PACIFIC RAILROAD BILL.

The following is an authentic copy of the Pacific Railroad Bill, as it passed both branches of Congress. It has since

I expect to maintain this contest until successful, or till I die, or am conquered, or my term expires, or Congress or the country forsakes me.

July 18, 1862

CHASE:

President Lincoln and the 37th Congress have been very busy implementing a wide-sweeping

Republican agenda for the United States and to take the war to a new level of urgency.

Over the past fortnight, the President has called for 300,000 new military volunteers, signed legislation to impose a 3 percent internal revenue tax on incomes in excess of $600, signed the Pacific Railroad Act to build a transcontinental railroad, approved a bill to donate public lands to states and territories for colleges of agriculture and mechanic arts, approved the Anglo-American treaty that suppresses African slave trade.

Yesterday, President Lincoln signed an act authorizing the seizure and confiscation of rebel property to quote, "suppress the insurrection and punish those guilty of treason and rebellion."

Congress further authorized conscription and acceptance of Negroes into military and naval services, a move which is sure to distance any hope of conciliation with Southern leaders.

BURKE: The tone is no different across the Confederacy, especially when people realized how many soldiers

were lost in the recent victories. There is widespread concern that the Confederate war strategy must change because the South cannot match the North in terms of men and materiel.

The *Charleston Mercury* demanded, "Our victorious troops in Virginia, reduced though they be in numbers, must be led promptly into Maryland."

Confederate leaders believe a successful invasion of the North might lead to Democratic gains in the upcoming elections and thereby weaken political support for the war effort.

DAVIS:

My early declared purpose and continued hope was to feed upon the enemy and teach them the blessings of peace by making them feel in its most intangible form the evils of war.

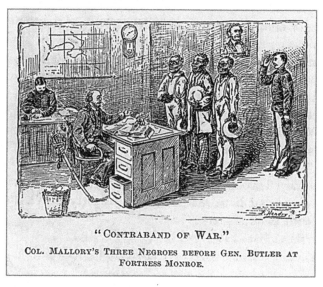

"CONTRABAND OF WAR."

COL. MALLORY'S THREE NEGROES BEFORE GEN. BUTLER AT FORTRESS MONROE.

The time and place for invasion has been a question of not of will but of power. Never having preferred defensive to offensive war, but rather pined for the day when our soil should be free from invasion and our banners float over the fields of the enemy, we stand upon the defensive no more.

When it is in our power to inflict injury upon our adversary, a proposal of recognition to the United States would show conclusively to the world that our sole object is the establishment of our independence and the attainment of an honorable peace.

The proposal of peace would enable the people of the United States to determine at their coming elections whether they will support those who favor a prolongation of the war or those who wish to bring it to termination.

* * * * *

DOUGLASS: Men have their choice in this world. They can be angels, or they may be demons. Just what takes place in individual human hearts, often takes place between nations, and between individuals of the same nation. Such is the struggle now going on in the United States. The slaveholders had rather reign in hell than serve in heaven.

To fight against slaveholders, without fighting against slavery, is but a half-hearted business, and paralyzes the hands engaged in it.

The strength of the rebels, the vigor with which they prosecute the war, the deadly hate towards the North, the employment of slaves to do the drudgery of the rebel army, and to shoot down the Government troops – the fact that this is a slaveholder's rebellion and nothing else – all point out slavery as the thing to be struck down as the best means of the successful and permanent establishment of the peace and prosperity of the nation.

Chapter 7 – The Prayer of Twenty Millions

*W*ith recent Union Army of the Potomac losses to Confederate forces led by General Robert E. Lee along the Virginia Peninsula and so close to Washington, DC, Northerners in both political parties have grown anxious. Mid-term elections are only a few months away. The Republican majority in both houses of Congress that has generally acceded to President Lincoln's appeals is at risk.

Appalling body counts are giving traction to the Democrats opposition to the war and support for peace with the South, even if that means the Confederacy achieves its independence and separation from the Union.

Radical Republicans and Abolitionists, who have had high hopes for the President since the election, increasingly feel the window of opportunity to act is closing. As such, they continue to apply public pressure for Mr. Lincoln to emancipate the slaves.

Ever cognizant of the need to keep the "border states" in the Union fold, Lincoln treads lightly in responding to an editorial by the influential Horace Greeley.

August 22, 1862

CHASE: President Lincoln responded to an open letter published in the *New York Tribune* on the 19th by its editor, Horace Greeley, titled "The Prayer of Twenty Millions." Greeley, who has been both supportive and critical of the President's actions, passionately called on the President to

THE PRAYER OF TWENTY MILL-
IONS.

To ABRAHAM LINCOLN, *President of the U. States:*

DEAR SIR: I do not intrude to tell you—for you must know already—that a great proportion of those who triumphed in your election, and of all who desire the unqualified suppression of the Rebellion now desolating our country, are sorely disappointed and deeply pained by the policy you seem to be pursuing with regard to the slaves of Rebels. I write only to set succinctly and unmistakably before you what we require, what we think we have a right to expect, and of what we complain.

declare emancipation for all slaves in Union-held territory.

Greeley wrote that it is "preposterous and futile to try to put down the rebellion without destroying slavery. The Union cause has suffered from a mistaken deference to Rebel slavery."

LINCOLN: If there be those who would not save the Union, unless they could at the same time save slavery, I do not agree with them. If there be those who would not save the Union unless they could at the same time destroy slavery, I do not agree with them. My paramount object in this struggle is to save the Union, and is not either to save or to destroy slavery.

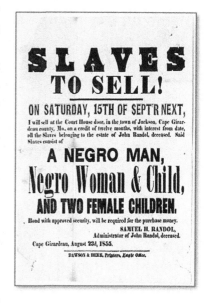

If I could save the Union without freeing any slave, I would do it, and if I could save it by freeing all the slaves, I would do it; and if I could save it by freeing some and leaving others alone, I would also do that.

What I do about slavery and the colored race, I do because I believe it helps to save the Union; and what I forbear, I forbear because I do not believe it would help to save the Union.

* * * * *

DOUGLASS: I come now to the policy of President Lincoln in reference to slavery. I do not undertake to say that the present administration has no policy, but if it has, the people have a right to know what it is, and to approve or disapprove of it, as they shall deem it wise or unwise.

Now the policy of an administration can be learned in two ways. The first by what it says, and the second by what it does, and the last is far more certain and reliable than the first.

Now what has been the tendency of his acts since he became Commander in chief of the army and navy?

He has scornfully rejected the policy of arming the slaves, a policy naturally suggested and enforced by the nature and necessities of the war. He has steadily refused to proclaim, as he had the constitutional and moral right to proclaim, complete emancipation to all the slaves of rebels who should make their way into the lines of our army.

He has repeatedly interfered with and arrested the anti-slavery policy of some of his most earnest and reliable generals. He has assigned to the most important positions, generals who are notoriously pro-slavery and hostile to the party and principles which raised him to power. He has permitted rebels to recapture their runaway slaves in sight of the capital.

It is from such action as this, that we must infer the policy of the Administration is simply and solely to reconstruct the Union on the old and corrupting basis of compromise, by which slavery shall retain all the power that it ever had, with the full assurance of gaining more, according to its future necessities.

Mr. Lincoln is powerful, Mr. Lincoln can do many things, but Mr. Lincoln will never see the day when he can bring back or charm back, the scattered fragments of the union into the shape and form they stood when they were shattered by this slaveholding rebellion.

Recognize the fact, for it is the great fact, and never more palpable than at the present moment that the only choice left to this nation is abolition or destruction. You must abolish slavery or abandon the union.

Chapter 8 – Antietam

*G*eneral Robert E. Lee's string of decisive victories on Southern soil brings confidence to the Confederate leadership that an invasion of the North will instill fear in the Union citizenry and sway public opinion before the mid-term election.

On his way north, Lee's plans to plans to divide his army into three units were lost and discovered by Union soldiers. Despite this advantage, McClellan cannot destroy Lee's army at Antietam, Maryland. The blood shed on a single day of fighting stuns the world.

September 18, 1862

ANDERSON: Earlier this year, the casualties at the battle of Shiloh eclipsed all others to that date, combined. This was followed by the Seven Days Battles where one quarter of the Union Army and one third of the Confederate Army were lost.

As shocking as it sounds, the fighting to date was merely a prelude to what was witnessed yesterday in the Maryland countryside of Antietam.

At daybreak, the fighting began as soon as the sun made its appearance over horizon. For the next three hours, thousands of men fired volleys of rifles and batteries of artillery raked the cornfield with grapeshot. Attack was met by counterattack, gains were followed by retreats.

Union forces achieved a break following a gallant charge of the Irish Brigade consisting of regiments of Irish immigrants from New York and Massachusetts. Advancing forward under the carry of a green flag with golden harp, the Irish troops fought their way to the sunken road and unleased a furious volley of fire at the defending Rebel soldiers. The road was filled with Confederate corpses so thick that a man could walk across the field without touching the earth beneath the bodies.

With the center of the Confederate line breached and the entire army in peril, General Lee reacted quickly by sending reserves into the line and halted the Union advance.

A new Union attack to the south sent Federal troops over a narrow stone bridge crossing the Antietam Creek. Awaiting on the other side of the bridge was a brigade of Georgians who positioned themselves on the bluffs overlooking the bridge.

From this favorable defensive position, they were able to hold off the Union assault for hours, until a heroic charge by New York and Pennsylvania troops took control of the bridge in the afternoon.

By nightfall, what remained of the countryside was a killing field, with bodies of men and horses several deep as far as the eye can see. It is estimated that 24,000 casualties were sustained on this single day of fighting.

This morning, General Lee prepared his weary troops for a new Federal assault that never came. A truce was secured to enable both sides to tend to those still alive. The battle was finally over when General Lee withdrew his troops across the Potomac, back to Virginia.

The Union victory, a pyrrhic one for sure, was aided by a prior discovery of the Confederate plans. For more on this, let's go to Jackie Chase in Washington, DC.

CHASE:

That is true, Carter. General Lee put his battle scheme on paper to coordinate his advancing columns. On September 13, a pair of Union infantrymen found an envelope containing three cigars and a paper. That paper turned out to be General Lee's Special Order #191, which exposed his risky plans to divide his army into units on each side of the Potomac.

Upon reading the plans, General McClellan is reported to have said, "Here is a paper with which if I cannot whip Bobbie Lee, I will be willing to go home."

General McClellan did defeat General Lee but he did not 'whip' him nor did he 'destroy Lee's army' as President Lincoln had hoped.

Despite knowing Lee's plans and commanding superior numbers, McClellan squandered the opportunity to destroy Lee's army and end the war.

He committed barely 50,000 infantry and artillerymen to the contest, and a third of his army did not fire a single shot. Though his men repeatedly drove the Army of Northern Virginia to the brink of disaster, exhibiting extraordinary feats of gallantry and heroism, McClellan allowed Lee to escape back to Virginia.

BURKE: Jackie, as you would expect, the Confederate retreat, though necessary, had to be painful for both General Lee and President Davis. The invasion of Maryland was a daring attempt to dramatically change the tenor of the war as well as better provide for their resource-deficient troops. The bountiful fields of Maryland and Union warehouses of shoes and supplies contributed to the decision. Moreover, a victory on Union soil could have hastened the war's end by garnering international recognition and stifling Northern support of the war.

However, as great were the possibilities, so too were the consequences.

Lee simply could not afford significant losses to his army - which is exactly what happened. Though Union casualties were greater in number, Confederate losses accounted for 31% of its total troop strength. General Lee had no choice but to withdraw to save his army for another day.

Chapter 9 – The Proclamation

*I*n his reply to Horace Greeley, President Lincoln cleverly introduced that, if he could save the Union by abolishing slavery, he would do so. Previously, the restoration of the Union and the abolition of slavery were widely viewed as separate, rather than interrelated, matters. Lincoln's conclusion points to a third way – abolish slavery in order to restore the Union.

President Lincoln uses the victory at Antietam, however marginal, to announce the Proclamation of Emancipation.

September 22, 1862

DOUGLASS: Common sense, the necessities of the war, to say nothing of the dictation of justice and humanity, have at last prevailed. We shout for joy that we live to record this righteous decree.

Important Proclamation by the President.

THE SLAVES OF REBELS PRO-CLAIMED FREE.

BY THE PRESIDENT OF THE UNITED STATES OF AMERICA:

A PROCLAMATION.

Abraham Lincoln, President of the United States, Commander-in-Chief of the army and navy, in his own peculiar, cautious, forbearing and hesitating way, slow, but we hope sure, has, while the loyal heart was near breaking with despair, proclaimed and declared: "That on the First of January, in the Year of Our Lord One Thousand, Eight Hundred and Sixty-three, All Persons Held as Slaves Within Any State or Any Designated Part of a State, The People Whereof Shall Then be in Rebellion Against the United States, Shall be Thenceforward and Forever Free."

"Free forever" oh! long enslaved millions, whose cries have so vexed the air and sky, suffer on a few more days in sorrow, the hour of your deliverance draws nigh!

Read the proclamation for it is the most important of any to which the President of the United States has ever signed his name.

His word has gone out over the country and the world, giving joy and gladness to the friends of freedom and progress wherever those words are read, and he will stand by them, and carry them out to the letter.

If he has taught us to confide in nothing else, he has taught us to confide in his word.

The President doubtless saw, as we see, that it is not more absurd to talk about restoring the union, without hurting slavery, than restoring the union without hurting the rebels. As to exasperating the South, there can be no more in the cup than the cup will hold, and that was full already.

The effect of this paper upon the disposition of Europe will be great and increasing. It changes the character of the war in European eyes and gives it an important principle as an object, instead of national pride and interest. It recognizes and declares the real nature of the contest, and places the North on the side of justice and civilization, and the rebels on the side of robbery and barbarism.

The South is thoroughly in earnest and confident. It has staked everything upon the rebellion. Its experience thus far in the field has rather increased its hopes of final success than diminished them. Its armies now hold us at bay at all points. The rebels confront us on the Potomac, the Ohio, and the Mississippi.

In short, we have yet, after eighteen months of war, scarcely more than touched the surface of the terrible evil.

Tenderness towards slavery has been the loyal weakness during the war. Fighting the slaveholders with one hand and holding the slaves with the other, has been fairly tried and has failed. We have now inaugurated a wiser and better policy, a policy which is better for the loyal cause than an hundred thousand armed men.

The Star Spangled Banner is now the harbinger of Liberty and the millions in bondage, inured to hardships, accustomed to toil, ready to suffer, ready to fight, to dare and to die, will rally under that banner wherever they see it gloriously unfolded to the breeze.

Let the black man have an arm as well as a heart in this war, and the tide of battle which has thus far only waved backward and forward, will steadily set in our favor. The rebellion suppressed, slavery abolished, and America will, higher than ever, sit as a queen among the nations of the earth.

Chapter 10 – The Mid-Terms

1862 is the first election since hostilities began. It occurs on the heels of Lincoln's Emancipation Proclamation in September. Republicans are anxious. Despite the nobleness of the Proclamation and the rhetoric of Abolitionists, the majority of whites in the North are still intolerant and fearful of what emancipation would mean to their own lives and livelihood. In the end, it could have been worse.

November 4, 1862

ANDERSON: This is Carter Anderson at the American News Network 1862 Mid-term Election Headquarters.

ABE LINCOLN'S LAST CARD; OR, ROUGE-ET-NOIR.

Republicans have been very uneasy about this election which comes less than two months after President Lincoln issued his Emancipation Proclamation. Almost immediately, Democrats made this election a referendum about abolitionism and white supremacy.

The New York Democratic platform described the Emancipation Proclamation as "a proposal for the butchery of women and children, for scenes of lust and rapine, and of arson and murder."

In Ohio, a Democratic newspaper editor was even more direct by writing, "A large majority can see no reason why they should be shot for the benefit of the niggers and Abolitionists."

Since taking office in the spring of 1861, President Lincoln has had a House and Senate dominated by Republicans, as seats of seceded Southern states have remained vacant. That will change in the New Year as Democrats registered significant gains in Pennsylvania, Ohio, Indiana, Illinois and New York. All will be sending new Democratic majorities to Congress.

Yet, these results do not tell the whole story. For that, let's go to Jackie Chase in Washington, DC.

CHASE: Carter, administration officials are certainly not pleased with the results but they also recognize it could have been worse.

The net loss of congressional seats is the smallest in 20 years, leaving Republicans still in control of the House with a 25-vote majority. In the Senate, Republicans actually gained five seats.

Word from inside the White House is that, in light of the results, President Lincoln has no intention of altering his policies and prosecution of the war.

LINCOLN: Fellow-citizens of the Senate and House of Representatives:

Since your last annual assembling, another year of health and bountiful harvests has passed. And while it has not pleased the Almighty to bless us with a return of peace, we can but press on, guided by the best light He gives us, trusting that in His own good time, and wise way, all will yet be well.

On the twenty-second day of September last, a proclamation was issued by the Executive.

Our strife pertains to ourselves - to the passing generations of men; and it can, without convulsion, be hushed forever with the passing of one generation.

Without slavery, the rebellion could never have existed; without slavery, it could not continue.

The dogmas of the quiet past are inadequate to the stormy present. The occasion is piled high with difficulty, and we must rise with the occasion. As our case is new, so we must think anew, and act anew. We must disenthrall ourselves and then we shall save our country.

Fellow-citizens, we cannot escape history. We of this Congress and this administration will be remembered in spite of ourselves. No personal significance, or insignificance, can spare one or another of us. The fiery trial through which we pass, will light us down, in honor or dishonor, to the latest generation.

We say we are for the Union. The world will not forget that we say this. We know how to save the Union. The world knows we do know how to save it. We - even we here - hold the power and bear the responsibility.

In giving freedom to the slave, we assure freedom to the free - honorable alike in what we give and what we preserve. We shall nobly save, or meanly lose, the last best hope of earth. Other means may succeed; this could not fail. The way is plain, peaceful, generous, just - a way which, if followed, the world will forever applaud, and God must forever bless.

Chapter 11 – Carousel of Generals

*W*hile the Confederate Army of Northern Virginia is commanded ably and consistently by General Robert E. Lee, President Lincoln is anything but satisfied with the leadership of the Union Army of the Potomac. With the mid-term election behind, Lincoln replaces General George B. McClellan, the darling of the Democratic Party who publicly stated his intention to become President, if not dictator. He turns to General Ambrose Burnside with the advice to aggressively pursue Lee. Burnside fails miserably and is replaced.

November 5, 1862

ANDERSON:

Less than 24 hours after the mid-term voting ended, President Abraham Lincoln relieved General George B. McClellan of his command of the Union Army of the Potomac. Given the popularity of "Little Napoleon", the President could not have taken this action before the election, despite his persistent frustration with the general's willingness to fight.

General McClellan was initially given command of the army after the loss at Bull Run in July 1861. McClellan quickly got to work providing the men with proper military training and instilling in them a remarkable *esprit de corps.* In recognition of organizing the army into an impressive fighting force, McClellan was given the title of General in Chief when Winfield Scott resigned.

McClellan quickly developed a reputation for his arrogance and contempt toward the political leaders in Washington, D.C. McClellan wrote privately that Lincoln was "nothing more than a well-meaning baboon," and that Secretary of State William Seward was an "incompetent little puppy."

Lincoln finally tired of McClellan's insults and removed him from title General in Chief in March of this year.

CHASE: Carter, were it not for the mid-terms, it is likely the President would have removed General McClellan after the battle at Antietam. Not only did the Union force outnumber the Confederates, but General Lee's battle plans were discovered by Union soldiers before the fight. Despite the troop advantage and the intelligence, McClellan barely left the field with a victory over Lee. McClellan also did not commit his full force in the battle, thereby allowing Lee to escape back to Virginia and fight another day.

When the President learned of this failure to fight and that McClellan overruled his field generals who requested the order to join the fighting, Lincoln was furious.

Many Republicans believe McClellan did not pursue Lee because of his antipathy towards emancipation. McClellan has said he "will not fight for abolitionists." McClellan, a Democrat, believes slavery is protected by the Constitution.

November 7, 1862

ANDERSON:

President Lincoln named Ambrose Burnside General of the Army of the Potomac today. The President asked Burnside, who reluctantly accepted the assignment, to immediately begin making aggressive plans to confront and destroy the Confederate army.

November 25, 1862

BURKE:

This is Danielle Burke reporting from Fredericksburg, Virginia on the shore of the Rappahannock River.

After being alerted to the movement of the Union Army, General Lee has shifted his Army of Northern Virginia from Richmond to the high ground outside of Fredericksburg. All of General Longstreet's corps have arrived and been placed on the western ridge known as Marye's Heights. General Jackson has his Second Corps troops marching 20 miles a day from Winchester to get here before Union troops cross the river.

December 13, 1862

CHASE:

Today began cold and overcast. A dense fog blanketed the ground and made it impossible for the armies to see each other. The weather, however, did not stop the fighting.

General Burnside, determined to display an aggressive spirit in his new role as Commander of the Army of the Potomac, ordered simultaneous attacks against Confederate forces, north and south of the city. A Union breakthrough by General Meade was wasted when 20,000 men remained standing in reserve. Skirmishing and artillery duels continued until dark, resulting in 5,000 Union and 3,400 Confederate casualties.

This lost opportunity was pre-empted by the fighting to the north. General Burnside ordered his commander of the Right Grand Division to send "a division or more" to seize the high ground to the west of the city.

BURKE: Jackie, about 600 yards to the west of Fredericksburg is a low ridge known as Marye's Heights, rising 40–50 feet above the plain. The ridge is protected by a 4-foot stone wall, enhanced in places with log breastworks and abatis, making it a perfect infantry defensive position.

Stationed there were 9,000 Confederate troops and sharpshooters, along with ample artillery. The Confederate artillery commander said "we cover that ground now so well that we will comb it as with a fine-tooth comb. A chicken could not live on that field when we open on it."

One would think this advantage would discourage any attack. Such was not the case.

A Federal brigade burst toward Marye's Heights and the stone wall, then another, and another, until three entire divisions had hurled themselves at the Confederate bastion. In one hour, the Army of the Potomac lost nearly 3,000 men; but the madness continued.

CHASE: Danielle, it is clear now that General Burnside either overestimated his forces or underestimated the enemy's position – or perhaps both – as more Union assaults tested the impossible.

Each blue wave crested short of the goal. Not a single Union soldier laid his hand on the stone wall.

One Federal soldier said, "Men fell like leaves in autumn. It seems miraculous that any of us escaped at all."

It was only when darkness shrouded the battlefield that, at last, the guns fell silent.

December 15, 1862

ANDERSON:

The White House received news this evening of a devastating loss at Fredericksburg.

Today, Federal forces retreated across the river, ending the Fredericksburg campaign in defeat. Casualties sustained by each army showed clearly how disastrous the Union army's tactics were. The Union Army sustained the loss of over 12,000 men, more than twice that lost by the Confederates.

The South erupted in jubilation over their great victory. *The Richmond Examiner* described it as a "stunning defeat to the invader, a splendid victory to the defender of the sacred soil."

Northern reaction has been fierce. *The Cincinnati Commercial* wrote, "It can hardly be in human nature for men to show more valor or generals to manifest less judgment, than were perceptible on our side."

Pennsylvania Governor Andrew Curtin told the president, "It was not a battle, it was butchery." Curtin reported that the president was "heart-broken at the recital."

January 26, 1863

CHASE:

This is Jackie Chase coming to you from the White House in Washington, DC.

After a disastrous and bloody defeat at Fredericksburg and a failed second offensive bogged down by winter rains, General Ambrose Burnside asked the President to have several officers, who were openly insubordinate, be relieved of duty and court-martialed.

Absent that, the General offered to resign.

Today, President Lincoln chose the latter option and replaced him with Maj. Gen. Joseph Hooker, one of the officers who had conspired against Burnside.

Chapter 12 – Emancipation Changes Everything

*L*incoln's Emancipation Proclamation is the gauntlet of the war. The war is no longer just about states' rights. Southern states will never return to the Union with slavery intact. The only way forward to ensure its way of life endures is through victory. Likewise, for the North, the war is no longer about preserving the Union but destroying the old south.

January 31, 1863

ANDERSON: In issuing the Proclamation, Mr. Lincoln made the abolition of slavery a war aim to save the Union.

The Emancipation Proclamation seeks to destroy an institution that has been an integral part of life in the South for over 200 years.

THE PET LAMB AND THE BLACK SHEEP; OR, THE UNHAPPY SHEPHERD.
Long Abe—"OH, THUNDER! HERE'S THAT DARNED BLACK SHEEP AGAIN!"

Thomas Jefferson said of slavery, "we have the wolf by the ear, and we can neither hold him, nor safely let him go. Justice is in one scale, and self-preservation in the other."

That wolf is now free and Southern society built on a foundation of slavery is now at risk of ruin – unless the Confederacy can achieve independence by defeating the Union on the battlefield.

In this sense, the fighting, which began in a most leisurely fashion at Bull Run, is now about total war – where the winner must crush the enemy to achieve its political goal – independence and the preservation of slavery for the South, reunification and abolition of slavery for the North.

Danielle Burke is in Richmond with reaction to the Proclamation in the South.

BURKE: Carter, the consensus among Southern leaders is that the 'old' Union is gone forever. If there were any illusions of a peaceful reconciliation with the North, they are now delusions.

BUTLER HANGED—THE NEGRO FREED—ON PAPER—1863.

This makes the fight for independence that much more urgent. The ante has been raised. The only way forward now to protect the Southern way of life is, as you said, to go 'all in' on the war, until there are no more Confederate soldiers left standing.

DAVIS: Citizens of the non-slaveholding States of America, heretofore, the warfare has been conducted by white men - peers, scions of the same stock; but the program has been changed, and your rulers despairing of a triumph by the employment of white men, have degraded you and themselves, by inviting the cooperation of the black race.

Now, therefore, as a compensatory measure, I do hereby issue the following Address to the People of the Non-Slaveholding States:

On and after February 22, 1863, all free Negroes within the limits of the Southern Confederacy shall be placed on slave status, and deemed to be chattels, they and their issue forever.

MONKEY UNCOMMON UP, MASSA!

All Negroes who shall be taken in any of the States in which slavery does not now exist, in the progress of our arms, shall be adjudged, immediately after such capture, to occupy the slave status, and in all States which shall be vanquished by our arms, all free Negroes shall, *ipsofacto*, be reduced to the condition of helotism, so that the respective normal conditions of the white and black races may be ultimately placed on a permanent basis, so as to prevent the public peace from being thereafter endangered.

Abraham Lincoln has seen fit to ignore the Constitution he has solemnly sworn to support, it ought not be considered polemically or politically improper in me to vindicate the position which has been at an early day of this Southern republic, assumed by the Confederacy, namely, that slavery is the corner-stone of a Western Republic.

CHASE: The reaction in the North to the Proclamation is split along party lines.

Senator Charles Sumner of Massachusetts exclaimed, "The skies are brighter and the air is purer, now that slavery has been handed over to judgment."

Senator Thaddeus Stevens of Pennsylvania hopes the slaves will be "incited to insurrection and give the rebels a taste of real civil war."

William Lloyd Garrison, the venerable abolitionist, called the occasion "a great historic event, sublime in its magnitude and beneficent in its far-reaching consequences."

However, anti-war Democratic papers sharply criticized the Proclamation as "insulting to God as to man, for it declares those 'equal' whom God created unequal."

The *Macomb Eagle* spelled it out in plainer terms, predicting that Lincoln and his ilk "will go flaming with the grand object of hugging niggers to their bosoms."

March 21, 1863

LINCOLN:

While commendation in newspapers and by distinguished individuals is all that a vain man could wish, the stocks have declined and troops come forward more slowly than ever. The North responds to the proclamation sufficiently in breath; but breath alone kills no rebels.

* * * * *

DOUGLASS:

When first the rebel cannon shattered the walls of Sumter and drove away its starving garrison, I predicted that the war then and there inaugurated would not be fought out entirely by white men. Every month's experience during these dreary years has confirmed that opinion.

A war undertaken and brazenly carried on for the perpetual enslavement of colored men, calls logically and loudly for colored men to help suppress it. Only a moderate share of sagacity was needed to see that the arm of the slave was the best defense against the arm of the slaveholder.

Hence, with every reverse to the national arms, with every exulting shout of victory raised by the slaveholding rebels, I have implored the imperiled nation to unchain against her foes, her powerful black hand. Slowly and reluctantly, that appeal is beginning to be heeded.

There are weak and cowardly men in all nations. We have them amongst us. They tell you this is the "white man's war"; that you will be "no better off after than before the war"; that the getting of you into the army is to "sacrifice you on the first opportunity."

Believe them not; cowards themselves, they do not wish to have their cowardice shamed by your brave example. Leave them to their timidity, or to whatever motive may hold them back.

I have not thought lightly of the words I am now addressing you. The counsel I give comes of close observation of the great struggle now in progress, and of the deep conviction that this is your hour and mine. In good earnest then, and after the best deliberation, I now for the first time during this war feel at liberty to call and counsel you to arms.

The case is before you. Let us win for ourselves the gratitude of our country, and the best blessings of our posterity through all time.

—————CB—————

Chapter 13 – Confederate Fortunes Rise

*B*eginning with the utterly disastrous defeat at Fredericksburg, the casualty rate of every new battle surpasses previous high water marks. With new enlistments falling rapidly, Lincoln and the War Department begin mustering free black men and former slaves into new 'colored' regiments. Frederick Douglass not only personally recruits enlistees but also contributes his two sons to the Massachusetts 54th. However, Union losses on the battlefield continue, including a masterful defeat of the Army of the Potomac by General Lee's Army of Northern Virginia at Chancellorsville, despite being outnumbered two-to-one.

April 1, 1863

ANDERSON: Last year ended when six Union divisions crossed an open field against a well-fortified Confederate line at Fredericksburg, causing such slaughter that Union General Ambrose Burnside wept openly at the outcome.

Along the Mississippi River, persistent efforts by the Union Army to take Vicksburg have come up short. The *Vicksburg Whig* gloats with the headline, "There is no immediate danger here."

DAVIS: One year ago many were depressed and some despondent. Now deep resolve is seen in every eye, an unconquerable spirit nerves every arm.

Recently, my friends, our cause has had the brightest sunshine to fall upon it, as well in the West as in the East. Our glorious Lee, the valued son, emulating the virtues of the

heroic Light-horse Harry, his father, has achieved a victory at Fredericksburg, and driven the enemy back from his last and greatest effort to get "on to Richmond." A few, I trust, may come from every battlefield to fulfil the pledge they made that they would come to Richmond - but they will come as captives, not as conquerors.

They have come to disturb your social organizations on the plea that it is a military necessity. For what are they waging war? They say to preserve the Union. Can they preserve the Union by destroying the social existence of a portion of the South? Do they hope to reconstruct the Union by striking at everything which is dear to man?

By showing themselves so utterly disgraced that if the question was proposed to you whether you would combine with hyenas or Yankees, I trust every Virginian would say, give me the hyenas.

ANDERSON: The absence of new progress by Union forces on the battlefields has given momentum to the Peace Democrats who say the South can never be conquered and that the only trophies of this war are "defeat, debt, and taxation."

Their answer to the war is to stop the fighting and start negotiations for reunion. As to the issue of slavery, the Peace Democrats say, "we should look only to the welfare, peace and safety of the white race, without reference to the effect that settlement may have on the African."

Jackie, time is not on the side of the Union. The longer this war drags on, the more difficult it will be for President Lincoln to wage war.

CHASE: Carter, that appears to be true. The Lincoln administration is genuinely concerned about the failure of Union forces – both in the west and the east – to follow up on the gains made in the fall of last year.

After replacing General McClellan following the election for not supporting the Emancipation Proclamation, Mr. Lincoln wasted no time in firing his replacement, General Burnside, for the costly defeat at Fredericksburg.

In the west, General Ulysses S Grant, who has amassed more battle victories than any other Union general, has gone as far as digging a canal that would reroute the Mississippi River in order to take Vicksburg. The combination of Vicksburg's natural defense and the Confederate garrison has proved superior to every maneuver he has employed in the campaign thus far.

DAVIS: If we can baffle them in their various designs this year, next fall there will be a great change in public opinion at the North. The Republicans will be destroyed  and the friends of peace will become strong. We have only therefore to resist manfully and our success will be certain.

LINCOLN: If there is a place worse than hell, I'm in it! We are now on the brink of destruction. It appears that the Almighty is against us.

April 10, 1863

ANDERSON: Though the Confederacy was formed on the principles of states' rights and sovereignty, President Davis has increasingly sought to centralize authority in order to effectively wage war.

A week ago, the Confederate leader addressed a crowd of hungry, desperate and violent women in Richmond who were protesting the high price of bread and food. Despite personnel pleas from Davis, the women broke into stores to loot food and supplies. It was not until Davis called in the bayonet-wielding militia did the women disperse.

Today, President Davis signed into Confederate law a bill limiting the cultivation of cotton and tobacco on private farms and plantations. Along with the Conscription Act and the imposition of an income tax, this bill is but another example of this contradictory phenomenon that has to haunt Davis and his administration as they seek to centralize authority in Richmond in a government founded on states' rights.

April 30, 1863

BURKE:

This is Danielle Burke with the Confederate Army of North Virginia under the command of General Robert E. Lee. Following the intense fighting in the Virginia Wilderness, General Lee met with General

Stonewall Jackson to plan their next move as they watch Federal troops under General Hooker move towards Richmond. With no Federal activity on the front, General Lee has scattered his forces to requisition provisions from the farmers and planters of North Carolina and Virginia.

CHASE: This is Jackie Chase on assignment with the Union Army of the Tennessee under the command of General Ulysses S. Grant. Today, General Grant sent his cavalry on a 600-mile expedition into the heart of Mississippi to tear up railroad lines supplying Vicksburg. He then had General William Tecumseh Sherman feign an attack north of the city, which enabled Grant to move 23,000 bluecoats across the River south of Vicksburg entirely unopposed by Confederate forces.

May 1, 1863

BURKE: When Federal scouts observed the movement of Stonewall Jackson's unit, they reported he was retreating. Instead, Jackson was in fact taking his 28,000 men along a 12-mile stretch of "hidden road" around the Union right flank. By nightfall, the Confederate Second Corps had advanced to within sight of Federal troops encamped at Chancellorsville.

CHASE: After crossing the Mississippi, General Grant's forces quickly overwhelmed 6,000 Rebel infantry at Port Gibson.

May 2, 1863

BURKE: Following the attack on the Union right flank, Stonewall Jackson sought to press his advantage before Union General Hooker and his army could regain their bearings and plan a counterattack. He rode out at night to determine the feasibility of a night assault by the light of the full moon, traveling beyond the farthest advance of his men.

As he and his staff returned, they were incorrectly identified as Union cavalry by men of the 18th North Carolina Infantry. Jackson was hit by three bullets, breaking his left arm which had to be amputated.

CHASE: General Sherman's unit joined that of General Grant, bringing the total troop strength to 40,000 east of Vicksburg. The men set out to forage for food among the many plantations of the Mississippi valley.

May 4, 1863

ANDERSON: The Union Army of the Potomac has suffered its greatest humiliation of the war this week at the battle of Chancellorsville. What should have been a grand victory turned into a disastrous defeat.

Despite greatly outnumbering its enemy more than two to one, and despite having the enemy surrounded on two sides, the Union army under General Joseph Hooker could not overcome the Rebel forces under their wily commander General Robert E. Lee.

All told, the fighting was some of the most furious anywhere in the war, as 21,357 men were lost, divided equally between the two armies.

LINCOLN:	Oh God, oh God. What will the country say?
DAVIS:	To General Lee: I have received your dispatch, and reverently unite with you in giving praise to God for the success with which He has crowned our arms.

CHANCELLORSVILLE.

In the name of the people, I offer my cordial thanks to yourself and the troops under your command for this addition to the unprecedented series of great victories which your army has achieved.

May 10, 1863

BURKE:

The Confederacy lost perhaps its most gifted military commander today when Thomas Jonathan "Stonewall" Jackson passed away from complications of pneumonia.

During the battle at Chancellorsville, Lt. Gen. Jackson was shot by Rebel pickets when he returned to camp after scouting the battlefield for advantageous positions.

It was Jackson's undetected maneuver around the right flank of the Union Army that initiated the Confederate offensive and eventual victory. The news stunned General Lee who has come to rely on the man they call Stonewall more than any other commander.

Chapter 14 – Races East and West

*I*n this the third year of the war, fighting is intensifying on both fronts. In the Western Theater, Grant relentlessly pursues Vicksburg knowing, with Northern morale falling, he cannot fail.

In the Eastern Theater, Lee seizes on his masterful victory at Chancellorsville to bring the fighting into Maryland and Pennsylvania, hoping to convince Europe that the Confederacy is deserving of recognition and their support.

May 14, 1863

CHASE: If Vicksburg is considered an 'immovable object,' then General Grant's Army of the Tennessee has to be considered an 'irresistible force.' Today, it demonstrated more of that quality as it easily captured the key transportation center of Jackson, Mississippi, thereby cutting Vicksburg off from the Confederacy and protecting its flank from attack as it turns its weaponry on the Rebel citadel.

In a demonstration of what General Grant refers to as 'total war,' Federal troops entered Jackson and burned part of the town and cut the railroad connections with Vicksburg. General Sherman ordered the destruction of all facilities that could benefit the war effort.

LINCOLN: We can take all the northern ports of the Confederacy, and they can defy us from Vicksburg. It means hog and hominy without limit, fresh troops from all the states of the far South, and a cotton country where they can raise the staple without interference. I am acquainted with that region and know what I am talking about, and, as valuable as New Orleans will be to us, Vicksburg will be more so.

May 15, 1863

BURKE:

General Lee traveled to Richmond to meet with President Davis and the Confederate Cabinet today to discuss strategy for the coming months. Though there are some reasons for optimism, overall, the future of the Confederacy, its ability to separate from the United States and be recognized globally as an independent sovereign nation, may come down to events both on the battlefield and in Europe that occur this summer.

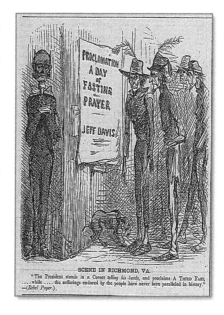

SCENE IN RICHMOND, VA.
"The President stands in a Corner, *telling his beads*, and proclaims A THIRD FAST, ...while .... the sufferings endured by the people have never been paralleled in history."
—*(Rebel Paper.)*

If the Confederacy is to gain Europe's recognition, it must do so soon. Even with the impressive victory at Chancellorsville, the Army of Northern Virginia lost a larger percentage of its available force than did the Union. The Conscription Act has helped but the continued control exerted by Confederate States over how many men they contribute to the national army has made it increasingly difficult for President Davis to replenish General Lee's Army.

Despite successes on the battlefield, the Southern economy has suffered badly over the past year. As states and the Confederacy have printed money to pay for the war effort and counter the economy's contraction, inflation has steadily worsened. Compounding the impact of inflation has been the prolonged drought in the South that has led to severe food shortages. The recent 'bread riots' in Richmond gave witness to this crisis.

The food shortages that have plagued the civilian economy of the South have also hit the armies in the field. Moreover, the vast majority of the fighting in the Eastern Theater has taken place in Northern Virginia.

The once bountiful and lush landscape is now barren. Where there were once trees, there are now stumps. Where there were once fields, there are now mud and shallow graves. Lee used to supplement his soldiers and horses' diet with local harvests. There are no more to be had.

May 22, 1863

CHASE:

After three weeks on the move, and two unsuccessful assaults to take the city by force, General Grant's army has set in for a siege on Vicksburg.

General Grant wanted to end it quickly and continue to maneuver against other enemies, but Vicksburg has defied every attack.

With artillery shells raining down on it from all sides, the only hope for the citizens of Vicksburg and the Rebel garrison inside is General Joseph Johnston's army now hovering near Jackson several dozen miles to the east.

June 21, 1863

BURKE:

Following his plan to invade the North, an infantry division of General Lee's Army of Northern Virginia arrived in Hagerstown, Maryland. The Washington Hotel is crowded with officers who pay $4 in Confederate money for a night's stay. Some troops have gone into Pennsylvania to bring back any Negroes they can find, who, they allege, ran away from their masters in Virginia.

June 22, 1863

CHASE:

Inside Vicksburg, citizens who remain and Confederate soldiers defending the city are coping as best as possible.

General Grant's army has been relentless in keeping the pressure on Vicksburg, ever extending their lines and tightening the noose around the beleaguered city to keep the Confederates from getting supplies of food or ordnance. Union soldiers have been digging various approach trenches toward Confederate lines, forcing Rebels to stay on the alert.

Union artillery from both land the river incessantly lob shells into the city. To escape the danger, residents have cut caves into the hillsides, some actually taking up residence there and foregoing their homes. During lulls in the artillery barrage, some will emerge from the caves and cellars to carry on seemingly 'normal' lives. But at the first sound of gunfire, they go scurrying for cover, and Vicksburg once more resembles a ghost town.

June 28, 1863

BURKE:

Confederate forces under General Lee continue to advance into Maryland and Pennsylvania, much to the fear and consternation of Northern citizens.

Local newspapers report that Union General Joseph Hooker was replaced with General George Meade as commander of the Army of the Potomac today. When General Lee was given the news, he said nothing then kicked his horse, Traveler, to move forward heading north.

July 1, 1863

CHASE: This is Jackie Chase with the Union Army of the Tennessee. General Grant's army has Vicksburg surrounded by land while Union warships under Admiral David Porter control the Mississippi River to the west. Between the two, they have bombarded the city essentially non-stop since the siege began in late May. As of today, Union approaches have reached the enemy's ditch at a number of places.

Orders have been given by General Grant to make all preparations for assault on the 6th of July.

DAVIS: Vicksburg must not be lost without a desperate struggle. The interest and the honor of the Confederacy forbid it. The eyes and hopes of the whole Confederacy are upon you.

BURKE: This is Danielle Burke with the Confederate Army of Northern Virginia as they move essentially without resistance into central Pennsylvania. General Lee has divided his army into three units, each going after an objective – one took Chambersburg, another went as far north as Harrisburg, and the third moved into Cashtown, just west of Gettysburg.

General Jubal Early moved through Gettysburg and demanded a ransom for the town, a pirate-like practice he had been performing as he traveled through towns, threatening to burn them down if they did not comply. They were given supplies from a train shipment that came through town. Apparently, the supplies were not enough, because a brigade was sent to ransack the town of shoes.

Chapter 15 – Joy and Despair

*T*win Union victories on the 4th of July propel the spirits of Northerners to new heights and of Southerners to new lows. Grant gets another "unconditional surrender" under his belt. With the capture of Vicksburg and the newly appointed General George Meade, he defeats Lee at Gettysburg with the help from some truly extraordinary heroics on his flanks: on the left flank at Little Round Top and on the right flank against a formidable Rebel cavalry charge.

Lee offers his resignation while Lincoln immortalizes the brave who gave their life, not for land, but for a principle, with 271 words in November.

July 4, 1863

ANDERSON: This is Carter Anderson with breaking news. On the day of its 87th birthday, the United States celebrates two extraordinary victories on the battlefield – one in Mississippi and the other in Pennsylvania.

First came the news of the surrender of Vicksburg to General Ulysses S. Grant, the city many regard as the most important prize on the Mississippi River.

President Lincoln called Vicksburg "the key to the Confederacy" and declared that the war could not be won "until the key is in our pocket." Today, that key was delivered into the Union pocket.

LINCOLN: The Father of Waters again goes unvexed to the sea. Grant is my man, and I am his, the rest of the war!

DAVIS: The clouds are truly dark over us. The disasters in Mississippi were both great and unexpected to me. But I have not yet seen cause to waver in the conviction to which I have frequently given expression, that, if our people now show as much fortitude as we are entitled to expect from those who display such conspicuous gallantry in the field, we shall certainly beat the enemy and secure our independence.

July 7, 1863

ANDERSON: For more on this story, let's go first to Danielle Burke in Richmond, and then to Jackie Chase in Washington, DC.

BURKE: Carter, the mood here is glum. The news from Vicksburg was all the more shocking because it was considered unassailable. The garrison there had little choice but to surrender. By late June, the situation was growing desperate. Disease was running rampant and people were starving. When

BY TELEGRAPH,
FOR THE AMERICAN & GAZETTE.

VICTORY!

PEMBERTON SURRENDERS

VICKSBURG UNCONDITIONALLY.

GETTYSBURG AND VICKSBURG
IN ONE DAY!!

the cannon fire stopped, residents came out of the holes dug into the hills to feast on rations provided by Union soldiers.

CHASE: Carter, not surprisingly, the atmosphere here in Washington is one of celebration. Two major victories on the 4th of July – the news could not be any better for President Lincoln.

These two victories come at an important time as public support for the war has fluctuated since the beginning of the year and recruitment efforts have become much more difficult.

When the general of the Vicksburg garrison asked General Grant for terms of surrender, Grant repeated what he said at Fort Donelson – "No terms except immediate and unconditional surrender."

29,495 Confederate soldiers were captured, paroled and allowed to go home.

Meanwhile, the victory at Gettysburg helps to erase the memories of the losses at Fredericksburg and Chancellorsville, both of which took many lives and demoralized the ranks of the Army of the Potomac.

A procession with bands of music proceeded to the Executive Mansion. The crowd enthusiastically cheered the President who appeared at an upper window and briefly spoke to the gathering.

LINCOLN: How long ago is it?---eighty odd years---since, on the Fourth of July for the first time in the history of the world, a nation by its representatives, assembled and declared as a self-evident truth that "all men are created equal."

Now, on this Fourth of July, when we have a gigantic Rebellion, at the bottom of which is an effort to overthrow the principle that all men were created equal, we have the surrender of a most powerful position and army on that very day.

BURKE: General Lee took the fighting to Gettysburg because, despite victories at Fredericksburg and Chancellorsville, the Army of Northern Virginia suffered huge losses during those battles.

Additionally, the grounds of Northern Virginia are devastated by continuous fighting and encamping. Food is scarce and forage nonexistent.

These factors convinced General Lee and President Davis that an invasion of the North, however

hazardous, was less risky than continuing to defend Richmond.

Another victory, within striking distance of Washington, Baltimore or even New York might have convinced Northerners and Europeans that the South could win, and deserved to win, its independence.

Lee's victory at Chancellorsville included a huge haul of captured weapons. After Chancellorsville, 90% of Lee's infantrymen were equipped with rifles instead of smoothbores. This increased Lee's confidence in the effectiveness of his infantry.

Lee's soldiers had overcome more daunting tasks at Gaines Mill, Sharpsburg and Chancellorsville. Gettysburg represented a chance to win the war.

After the loss at Gettysburg, General Lee offered his resignation to President Davis.

DAVIS: Where am I to find that new commander who possesses the greater ability which you believe is required? If Providence would kindly offer such a person for our use, I would not hesitate to avail of his services.

To ask me to substitute you by someone in my judgment more fit to command, or who would possess more of the confidence of the army or of the reflecting men in the country, is to demand for me an impossibility.

CHASE: The victory at Gettysburg came with an enormous price – for both sides.

Any one anxious about the definition of the word 'glory' will find the answer at Gettysburg. It is very beautiful, rolling country here. But, for five miles around, there is an awful smell of putrefaction.

One of the most revolting features of the field of battle is the large number of dead horses scattered over it. No effort has yet been made to bury them.

At a field hospital, the first sight that meets the eye is a collection of semi-conscious but still living human forms, all of whom shot through the head and considered hopeless. Yet they groan and their limbs toss and twitch.

A long table stood in the woods and around it gathered a number of surgeons and attendants. This is the operating table. A wagon stood near, rapidly filling with amputated legs and arms. Then, wholly filled, this gruesome spectacle withdrew from sight and returned for another load.

November 19, 1863

ANDERSON:

Today, President Lincoln visited the battlefield that witnessed the loss of over 50,000 Union and Confederate soldiers.

In the aftermath of the three-day carnage that took place in early July, the hamlet of Gettysburg found itself surrounded by thousands of bloating corpses. Soon after the battle, torrential rain exposed the bodies lying in hastily prepared shallow graves. The arrival of summer's humid heat brought with it the nauseating stench of decaying flesh that attracted swarms of flies and marauding pigs. The bodies of the fallen had to be given a proper internment.

The reburial of Union soldiers from the battlefield graves began on October 17. The committee for the

Consecration of the National Cemetery at Gettysburg invited President Lincoln to "formally set apart these grounds to their sacred use by a few appropriate remarks."

LINCOLN:

Four score and seven years ago, our fathers brought forth on this continent, a new nation, conceived in Liberty, and dedicated to the proposition that all men are created equal.

Now we are engaged in a great civil war, testing whether that nation, or any nation so conceived and so dedicated, can long endure. We are met on a great battle-field of that war.

We have come to dedicate a portion of that field, as a final resting place for those who here gave their lives that that nation might live.

It is altogether fitting and proper that we should do this.

But, in a larger sense, we cannot dedicate—we cannot consecrate—we cannot hallow—this ground. The brave men, living and dead, who struggled here, have consecrated it, far above our poor power to add or detract.

The world will little note, nor long remember what we say here, but it can never forget what they did here. It is for us the living, rather, to be dedicated here to the unfinished work which they who fought here have thus far so nobly advanced.

It is rather for us to be here dedicated to the great task remaining before us—that from these honored dead we take increased devotion to that cause for which they gave the last full measure of devotion—that we here highly resolve that these dead shall not have died in vain—that this nation, under God, shall have a new birth of freedom—and that government of the people, by the people, for the people, shall not perish from the earth.

Chapter 16 – Abolition or Union

*C*onfidence in Jefferson Davis begins to wane. The loss of Vicksburg is a huge blow to the Confederacy. In the North, the debate over the war's objective continues. Lincoln defends his policies as the only way to save the Union. Democrats insist the war is about Abolitionism and therefore not worth the cost.

February 1, 1864

DOUGLASS: I am one of those who believe that it is the mission of this war to free every slave in the United States. I am one of those who believe that we should consent to no peace which shall not be an Abolition peace. I look upon slavery as going the way of all the earth. It is the mission of the war to put it down.

DAVIS: I have seen no action that does not indicate the purpose of the enemy is to refuse all terms to the South except absolute, unconditional subjugation or extermination. Have we not just been apprised by that despot that we can only expect his gracious pardon by emancipating all our slaves, swearing allegiance and obedience to him and his proclamations, and becoming in point of fact the slaves of our own Negroes?

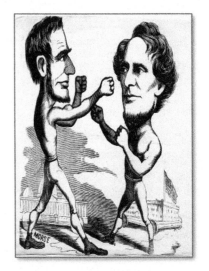

DOUGLASS: Protest, affirm, hope, glorify as

we may, it cannot be denied that Abolitionism is still unpopular in the United States. It cannot be denied that this war is at present denounced by its opponents as an Abolition war; and it is equally clear that it would not be denounced as an Abolition war, if Abolitionism was not odious.

I hold that it is an Abolition war, because slavery has proved itself stronger than the Constitution; it has proved itself stronger than the Union; and has forced upon us the necessity of putting down slavery in order to save the Union, and in order to save the Constitution.

I therefore call this just what the Democrats have charged it with being, an Abolition war.

LINCOLN: There are those who are dissatisfied with me. To such I would say: You desire peace; and you blame me that we do not have it.

But how can we attain it? There are but three conceivable ways. First, to suppress the rebellion by force of arms. This, I am trying to do. Are you for it? If you are, so far we are agreed.

If you are not for it, a second way is to give up the Union. I am against this. Are you for it? If you are, you should say so plainly.

If you are not for force, nor yet for dissolution, there only remains some imaginable compromise.

I do not believe any compromise, embracing the maintenance of the Union, is now possible. All I learn leads to a directly opposite belief.

To be plain, you are dissatisfied with me about the Negro. Quite likely, there is a difference of opinion between you and myself upon that subject. I certainly wish that all men could be free, while I suppose you do not. Yet I have neither adopted, nor proposed any measure, which is not consistent with even your view, provided you are for the Union.

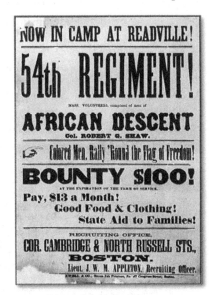

You dislike the Emancipation Proclamation; and, perhaps, would have it retracted. You say it is unconstitutional — I think differently. I think the constitution invests its commander-in-chief, with the law of war, in time of war.

The war has certainly progressed as favorably for us, since the issue of the proclamation, as before. I know as fully as one can know the opinions of others, that some of the commanders of our armies in the field, who have given us our most important successes, believe the emancipation policy, and the use of colored troops, constitute the heaviest blow yet dealt to the rebellion.

You say you will not fight to free Negroes. Some of them seem willing to fight for you.

Fight, then, exclusively to save the Union. I issued the proclamation on purpose to aid you in saving the Union.

March 1, 1864

ANDERSON:

There is also a growing peace movement in the South. No less than the Confederate Vice President Alexander Stephens, reacted angrily when the lame-duck session of Congress authorized President Davis to suspend the writ of habeas corpus, stating, "The bill is a blow at the very vitals of liberty. Far better that our country should be overrun by the enemy, our cities sacked and burned, and our land laid desolate, than the people should thus suffer the citadel of their liberties to be entered and taken by professed friends."

For more on these developments, let's go to Danielle Burke in Richmond.

BURKE:

Carter, there are quite a few high-ranking Southern politicians who fear the war is already lost and that Davis' policies of conscription, impressment, military despotism and economic ruin represent a greater threat to Southerners than a reunion with the United States.

Of course, President Davis will have none of such talk.

DAVIS: The advent of peace will be hailed with joy. Our desire for it has never been concealed. But, earnest as has been our wish for peace, and great as have been our sacrifices and sufferings during the war, the determination of this people has, with each succeeding month, become more unalterably fixed to endure any suffering, and continue any sacrifice, however prolonged, until their right to self-government, and the sovereignty and independence of these States, shall have been triumphantly vindicated and established.

The sole resource for us as a people secure in the justice of our cause, and holding our liberties to be more precious than all other earthly possessions, is to combine and apply every available element of power for their defense and preservation.

ℂℋ

Chapter 17 – Grant Comes East

*T*he *upcoming 1864 Presidential election is as important for the Confederacy as it is for Lincoln. With resources and manpower running thin, the best chance for Confederate independence may lie in the defeat of Abraham Lincoln.*

Lincoln's prospects for re-election are directly related to battlefield success. To bring that success to the Eastern Theater, Lincoln brings Grant from the West after he saves the day for a trapped Union army at Nashville. Grant leaves his Army of the Tennessee in the hands of William T. Sherman. The Northern public expects Grant and Sherman to immediately conquer the South and end the war. However, Lee is still in command in the East and Sherman has a long way to go to reach Atlanta.

March 10, 1864

ANDERSON: President Lincoln today officially promoted Major General Ulysses S. Grant to the rank of lieutenant general of the U.S. Army. The rank of lieutenant general was last used in 1798 when President John Adams assigned the post to former President George Washington in anticipation of a possible French invasion of the United States.

General Grant has distinguished himself from the beginning of the war by methodically capturing Rebel forts and cities along the Mississippi River

Valley, then capturing the Confederate citadel of Vicksburg in July of last year.

When Union forces were surrounded at Chattanooga in September, Lincoln gave Grant control of all Union armies in the West. After a 60-mile trip overland, in which soldiers at times had to carry him when he was unable to walk those stretches, he arrived in Chattanooga soaked to the skin on the evening of October 23.

He first reopened a supply line to the beleaguered Union Army then captured Lookout Mountain on November 24 before directing his forces to a stunning victory at Missionary Ridge the next day.

When news of the victory reached the Northern public, General Ulysses S. Grant became an instant celebrity – and, for some, a possible candidate for the Republican nomination.

Jackie Chase picks up the story from there.

CHASE: Carter, it is General Grant's immense popularity that gave the President pause in promoting him. When General Grant rode to the rescue at Chattanooga, rumors surfaced that many Northern senators were considering nominating Grant instead of Lincoln at the 1864 Republican National Convention.

It was only after General Grant issued a statement that he was not interested in any political candidacy did the President agree to promote Grant to the revived rank of lieutenant general of the U.S. Army.

On the evening of March 8, the President and Mrs. Lincoln gave a public reception at the White House.

At about half-past nine o'clock a sudden commotion near the entrance to the room attracted attention as General Grant walked along modestly with the rest of the crowd toward Mr. Lincoln. With a face radiant with delight, the President advanced rapidly toward his distinguished visitor.

Grant's right hand grasped the lapel of his coat; his head bent slightly forward, and his eyes upturned toward Lincoln's face. The President, eight inches taller, looked down with beaming countenance upon his guest.

LINCOLN: The nation's appreciation of what you have done, and it's reliance upon you for what remains to do, in the existing great struggle, are now presented with this commission, constituting you Lieutenant General in the Army of the United States.

April 12, 1864

CHASE: Carter, we have just received word of a terrible massacre of colored Union soldiers at Fort Pillow on the Tennessee bank of the Mississippi, 40 miles north of Memphis. Some 3,000 rebels under the command of Nathan Bedford Forrest stormed the fort held by a garrison of 600 Federal soldiers, roughly evenly divided between United States Colored Artillery regiments and white Unionists from East Tennessee.

When the Rebels scaled the walls, Union soldiers ran for the bluffs and the river but Confederate soldiers cut them off. A Northern surgeon watched helplessly as the Rebels lined up Federals for execution and hacked and shot the wounded.

A witness described the river as "dyed with the blood of the slaughtered for 200 yards."

April 18, 1864

LINCOLN:

When the war began, three years ago, neither party, nor any man, expected it would last till now. Each looked for the end, in some way, long ere to-day. Neither did any anticipate that domestic slavery would be much affected by the war.

But here we are; the war has not ended, and slavery has been much affected - how much needs not now to be recounted. So true is it, that man proposes, and God disposes.

A painful rumor, true I fear, has reached us of the massacre, by the rebel forces, at Fort Pillow, in the West end of Tennessee, on the Mississippi river, of some three hundred colored soldiers and white officers, who had just been overpowered by their assailants.

There seems to be some anxiety in the public mind whether the government is doing its duty to the colored soldier, and to the service, at this point. At the beginning of the war, and for some time, the use of colored troops was not contemplated; and how the change of purpose was wrought, I will not now take time to explain. Upon a clear conviction of duty, I resolved to turn that element of strength to account; and I am responsible for it to the American people, to the Christian world, to history, and on my final account to God.

Having determined to use the Negro as a soldier, there is no way but to give him all the protection given to any other soldier. The difficulty is not in stating the principle, but in practically applying it. It is a mistake to suppose the government is indifferent to this matter, or is not doing the best it can in regard to it.

If there has been the massacre of three hundred there, or even the tenth part of three hundred, the retribution, shall as surely come.

May 3, 1864

ANDERSON: The long awaited battle between Generals Lee and Grant commenced eight days ago in the Virginia Wilderness when the Army of the Potomac crossed the Rappahannock.

Since then, the struggle has been carried on with a fierceness and desperation unprecedented in the conflict thus far, if that can be believed after the carnage witnessed at Shiloh, Antietam and Gettysburg.

It is difficult to determine which side has been the most successful, though it is plainly evident that the Union has suffered the greater casualties.

We have to mourn the loss of many brave officers and men."

CHASE: Citizens across the North crowd newspaper and telegraph offices for any word on the contest. When General Grant declared in a dispatch to Washington, – "I propose to fight it out on this line if it takes all summer" – it made instant headlines. Everyone seems to think that Grant will enter Richmond and end the war before the autumn leaves begin to fall.

May 24, 1864

LINCOLN: The people are too sanguine. They expect too much at once. There is a great deal still to be done.

CHASE: In the past, when Union generals lost a battle to General Lee, they retreated to regroup and fight another day. Not so for General Grant. Three times his army was beaten by Lee's, yet he did not retreat. Instead, he moved south – always south toward Richmond, around Lee's right flank.

June 30, 1864

ANDERSON: Today Maryland's Constitutional Convention voted to abolish slavery. However, this favorable news to the Lincoln administration is overshadowed by the implausible loss of life and limb in the incessant fighting ongoing in Virginia between the two armies under Generals Lee and Grant.

In just six weeks at the Wilderness, Spotsylvania and Cold Harbor, General Grant has lost nearly two-thirds of the accumulated loss sustained during the past three years!

Jackie, how is the Lincoln Administration responding to these staggering casualty reports?

CHASE: Carter, the news is difficult for anyone to reconcile.

Secretary Seward perhaps said it best, "It seems like exaggeration that in describing conflict after conflict

in this energetic campaign, I am required always to say of the last one that it was the severest battle of the war."

Unfortunately, the news is not any better for General William T. Sherman who, after moving swiftly through northern Georgia in May, has met resistance on the outskirts of Atlanta.

Even Lincoln's allies are wilting with weariness. Horace Greeley, editor of the New York Tribune, wrote to the President, "Our bleeding, bankrupt, almost dying country longs for peace, shudders at the prospect of fresh conscriptions, of further wholesale devastations, and of new rivers of human blood."

July 17, 1864

BURKE:

Under a flag of truce, two Northerners met with President Jefferson Davis and Judah Benjamin in Richmond today to discuss the possibility of peace and reconciliation.

DAVIS:

I desire peace as much as you do. I deplore bloodshed as much as you do; but I feel that not one drop of the bloodshed in this war is on my hands; and I look up to my God and say this. I tried all in my power to avert this war. I saw it coming, and

PEACE.
MEETING OF HORACE GREELEY AND JEFF DAVIS AT RICHMOND.

for twelve years, I worked night and day to prevent it, but I could not.

We are not fighting for Slavery. We are fighting for independence, and that or extermination we will have.

If your papers tell the truth, it is your capital that is in danger, not ours. Some weeks ago, Grant crossed the Rapidan to whip Lee and take Richmond. And what is the net result?

Grant has lost seventy-five or eighty thousand men -- more than Lee had at the outset -- and is no nearer Richmond than at first; and Lee, whose front has never been broken, holds him completely in check, and has men enough to spare to invade Maryland and threaten Washington!

Sherman, to be sure, is before Atlanta; but suppose he is, and suppose he takes it? You know that the further he goes from his base of supplies the weaker he grows and the more disastrous defeat will be to him. And defeat may come. So, in a military view, I should certainly say our position was better than yours.

But if we were without money, without food, without weapons -- if our whole country were devastated, and our armies crushed and disbanded -- could we, without giving up our manhood, give up our right to govern ourselves? Would you not rather die, and feel yourself a man, than live, and be subject to a foreign Power?

We seceded to rid ourselves of the rule of the majority, and this would subject us to it again.

Amnesty, Sir, applies to criminals. We have committed no crime. You have emancipated nearly two million of our slaves, and if you will take care of them, you may emancipate the rest. I had a few when the war began. I was of some use to them; they never were of any to me.

Against their will, you 'emancipated' them, and you may 'emancipate' every Negro in the Confederacy, but we will be free! We will govern ourselves. We will do it if we have to see every Southern plantation sacked and every Southern city in flames.

Say to Mr. Lincoln from me that I shall at any time be pleased to receive proposals for peace on the basis of our independence. It will be useless to approach me with any other.

Chapter 18 – Lincoln under Pressure

*G*rant *dogs Lee at great loss of life and limb. Sherman moves towards Atlanta but gains are few. When results are not so quickly forthcoming, the Peace Democrats step up their white supremacy rhetoric and viciously attack Lincoln. By mid-summer, Lincoln is under enormous pressure from many angles, including his supporters, to drop emancipation as a war aim. Lincoln wavers but does not fall. In doing so, he expects to lose in November.*

July 30, 1864

ANDERSON: In an effort to cut Grant's supply lines and draw troops away from the Union army surrounding him at Petersburg, General Lee sent Jubal Early on a romp through the Shenandoah Valley, southern Pennsylvania and western Maryland. He held the Maryland communities of Hagerstown and Frederick hostage, agreeing to spare them only when they had paid him a total of $220,000.

On July 11, Early got to Silver Spring, Maryland, at the very edge of Washington DC, where he burned down the postmaster general's house. Today, his men torched Chambersburg, Pennsylvania, when it refused to pay a half-million dollars in protection money.

CHASE: Carter, the bad news just keeps coming for the North. Back at Petersburg, Union forces exploded 8,000 pounds of gunpowder into a tunnel dug under Confederate lines, creating a 30-foot deep hole.

Federal troops quickly moved into the crater but were trapped by its high walls and the frenzy of the rush. Rebels opened fire on the defenseless men and killed any Negro soldier who attempted to surrender. Union losses totaled 4,000.

August 17, 1864

LINCOLN: General Grant: I have seen your dispatch expressing your unwillingness to break your hold where you are. Neither am I willing. Hold on with a bulldog grip, and chew and choke, as much as possible.

August 19, 1864

ANDERSON: As the casualties pile up, Mr. Lincoln's political fortunes are fading fast. Pressure is building on him to drop emancipation as a condition for peace and to negotiate an end to the war.

Henry J. Raymond, chairman of the Republican National Committee, told the President: "The tide is setting strongly against us. Two special causes are assigned to this great reaction in public sentiment —

the want of military success, and the impression that we can have peace with Union, but you are fighting not for Union but for the abolition of slavery."

LINCOLN: I don't think it is personal vanity, or ambition - but I cannot but feel that the weal or woe of this great nation will be decided in the approaching canvas.

There are now between one and 200 thousand black men now in the service of the Union. Abandon all the posts now possessed by black men, surrender all these advantages to the enemy, and we would be compelled to abandon the war in three weeks.

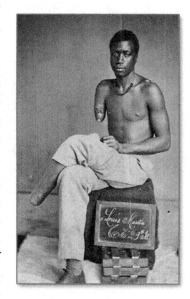

There have been men who have proposed to me to return to slavery the black warriors of Port Hudson and Olustee to their masters to conciliate the South. I should be damned in time and in eternity for so doing. The world shall know that I will keep my faith to friends and enemies, come what will.

My enemies say I am now carrying on this war for the sole purpose of abolition. It is and will be carried on so long as I am President for the sole purpose of restoring the Union.

But no human power can subdue this rebellion without using the Emancipation lever as I have done. Freedom has given us the control of 200,000 able-bodied men, born and raised on southern soil. It will give us more yet.

My enemies condemn my emancipation policy. Let them prove by the history of this war, that we can restore the Union without it.

August 24, 1864

CHASE:

It appears that President Lincoln would rather lose the election than lose his moral code by abandoning the war aim of emancipation. Yesterday, he asked each of his cabinet members to sign the back of an envelope, contents unseen. Many in the administration assume they were signing their resignations, as the prevailing consensus in Washington right now is that George McClellan will win in November.

Chapter 19 – War is Cruelty

As it happened several times before, the winds of the war shifted and gave lift to the Union fortunes. While Grant held Lee in check, Sherman finally took Atlanta. It appeared that a genuine corner in the conflict had finally been turned.

Almost immediately thereafter, the 'other' general Grant took from the West, Philip Sheridan, showed the Confederates and the World that the U.S. now had a first-rate cavalry. Sheridan began to employ the same tactics Sherman used in the South – destroy the means that support the fight – in the Shenandoah Valley. Between the two, the "cruelty of war" was delivered to the doorsteps of the Southern populace.

September 2, 1864

ANDERSON:

This just in to the ANN newsroom. Minutes ago, the War Department received a telegram from Union General William Tecumseh Sherman that read, "Atlanta is ours, and fairly won."

General Sherman's troops marched into the city, flags flying and bands playing yesterday after Confederate General John Hood evacuated Atlanta the day before.

Upon meeting Atlanta's mayor, General Sherman said, "War is cruelty and you cannot

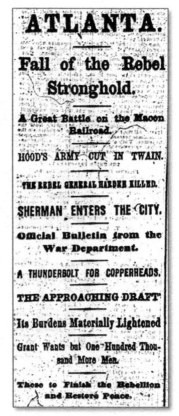

ATLANTA.

Fall of the Rebel Stronghold.

A Great Battle on the Macon Railroad.

HOOD'S ARMY CUT IN TWAIN.

THE REBEL GENERAL HARDEE KILLED.

SHERMAN ENTERS THE CITY.

Official Bulletin from the War Department.

A THUNDERBOLT FOR COPPERHEADS.

THE APPROACHING DRAFT

Its Burdens Materially Lightened

Grant Wants but One Hundred Thousand More Men.

These to Finish the Rebellion and Restore Peace.

refine it." His men then put a torch to everything of military value.

Jackie Chase is in Washington with the latest.

CHASE: Carter, it is hard to believe that just two weeks ago the mood here in Washington was all doom and gloom. The public's reaction to the news of Atlanta's fall was swift and nothing short of stunning.

The *New York Times'* lead story reads, "The victory is of such wide scope, such far-reaching result, such indisputable importance, that the country could do nothing but exult and look forward to the successful resolution of the war."

October 1, 1864

ANDERSON: When Confederate General Jubal Early attacked Union forces near Washington and raided several towns in Pennsylvania, Union General Grant created the Army of the Shenandoah and put General Philip Sheridan in charge. His assignment was to not only defeat Early's army but to lay waste to the Shenandoah Valley, which serves as the Confederate "breadbasket."

CHASE: Carter, General Grant told Sheridan, "Give the enemy no rest. Do all the damage to railroads and crops you can. Carry off stock of all descriptions and Negroes so as to prevent further planting. If the war is to last another year, we want the Shenandoah Valley to remain a barren waste."

After defeating General Early at Third Winchester and again at Fisher's Hill, General Sheridan did just as he was ordered and began "The Burning" – destroying barns, mills, railroads, factories – making over 400 square miles of the Valley uninhabitable.

BURKE: Here in Richmond, the value of the Confederate dollar has fallen to two percent of its 1861 level. The Confederate War Bureau revealed that the last meat ration has been issued to General Lee's army and not a pound remains in Richmond.

President Jefferson Davis traveled to Macon, Georgia today to appeal to the citizenry to join the war effort. In particular, the President chastised those who have abandoned the front and returned home as well as those who have used their wealth to avoid conscription.

DAVIS: Ladies and Gentlemen, Friends and Fellow-Citizens:

It would have gladdened my heart to have met you in prosperity instead of adversity. But friends are drawn together in adversity.

Though misfortune has befallen our arms from Decatur to Jonesboro', our cause is not lost. It does not become us to revert to disaster. "Let the dead bury the dead." Let us with one arm and one effort endeavor to crush Sherman. The end must be the defeat of our enemy.

The man who can speculate ought to be made to take up his musket. When the war is over and our independence won – and we will establish our independence – who will be our aristocracy? I hope the limping soldier.

To the young ladies I would say when choosing between an empty sleeve and the man who had remained at home and grown rich, always take the empty sleeve.

You have not many men between 18 and 45 left. The boys - God bless the boys - are, as rapidly as they become old enough, going to the field.

If one-half the men now absent without leave will return to duty, we can defeat the enemy. With that hope, I am going to the front. I may not realize this hope, but I know there are men there who have looked death in the face too often to despond now. Let no one despond. Let no one distrust, and remember that if genius is the beau ideal, hope is the reality.

Chapter 20 – A Second Term

*S*uccess on the battlefield sealed Lincoln's re-election and gave him the mandate to press the fight and abolish slavery forever with the 13th Amendment. Lincoln confirms his commitment to restoring the Union and abolishing slavery, effectively ending all speculation – both North and South – that the 'old,' divided United States will return.

November 8, 1864

ANDERSON: This is Carter Anderson with the American News Network Election Night Coverage, 1864. When Union battlefield losses and casualties escalated during the summer months, it then seemed impossible that Abraham Lincoln would be reelected. However, the capture of Atlanta and success in the Shenandoah Valley propelled the President to victory.

While the popular vote margin was only 400,000, the President's Electoral College tally represents a landslide, 212 to 21.

CHASE: Carter, the President's secretary said that Mr. Lincoln's pleasure from the election consists in the belief that the policy he has pursued is the best and only one that can save the country.

The President then reminded his cabinet members of August 23 when

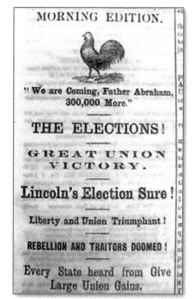

MORNING EDITION.

" We are Coming, Father Abraham, 300,000 More."

THE ELECTIONS!

GREAT UNION VICTORY.

Lincoln's Election Sure !

Liberty and Union Triumphant !

REBELLION AND TRAITORS DOOMED !

Every State heard from Give Large Union Gains.

he said it was exceeding probable that he would not be reelected and gave each of them a sealed envelope to sign. Tonight, he unsealed those envelopes for them to read the memo inside.

LINCOLN: This morning, as for some days past, it seems exceedingly probable that this Administration will not be re-elected. Then it will be my duty to so cooperate with the President elect, as to save the Union between the election and the inauguration; as he will have secured his election on such ground that he cannot possibly save it afterwards.

CHASE: At that time, the President was under heavy pressure from all sides, particularly his own allies, to abandon emancipation in favor of peace to end the war and restore the Union. By remaining true to his convictions and promise to the slave, Mr. Lincoln gained redemption tonight. It is fair to say that the United States is, for as long as Abraham Lincoln is president, irrevocably committed to a dual policy of unconditional surrender and emancipation.

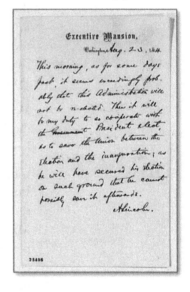

December 6, 1864

LINCOLN: Since the last annual message all the important lines and positions then occupied by our forces have been maintained, and our arms have steadily advanced.

At the last session of Congress a proposed amendment of the Constitution abolishing slavery throughout the United States, passed the Senate, but failed for lack of the requisite two-thirds vote in the House of Representatives. I venture to recommend the reconsideration and passage of the measure at the present session.

On careful consideration of all the evidence accessible, it seems to me that no attempt at negotiation with the insurgent leader could result in any good. He would accept nothing short of severance of the Union - precisely what we will not and cannot give.

His declarations to this effect are explicit and oft repeated. He does not attempt to deceive us. He affords us no excuse to deceive ourselves. He cannot voluntarily reaccept the Union; we cannot voluntarily yield it.

Between him and us, the issue is distinct, simple, and inflexible. It is an issue which can only be tried by war, and decided by victory. If we yield, we are beaten; if the Southern people fail him, he is beaten. Either way, it would be the victory and defeat following war.

I repeat the declaration made a year ago, that "while I remain in my present position I shall not attempt to retract or modify the emancipation proclamation, nor shall I return to slavery any person who is free by the terms of that proclamation, or by any of the Acts of Congress."

If the people should, by whatever mode or means, make it an Executive duty to re-enslave such persons, another, and not I, must be their instrument to perform it.

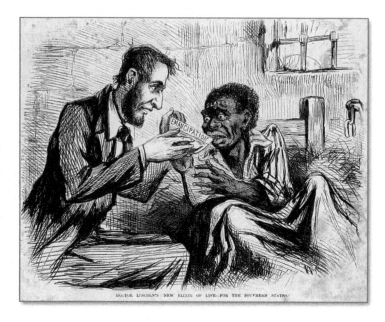

DOCTOR LINCOLN'S NEW ELIXIR OF LIFE—FOR THE SOUTHERN STATES.

Chapter 21 – Beginning of the End

*I*f there was one event that signaled the end was near, it was Sherman's March to the Sea. His 60,000-man army mowed through Georgia, essentially unopposed, destroying everything along the way that could lend support to the Confederate war effort. Terror and demoralization reigned in his path and in his wake. Lee could do nothing as he was paralyzed under a siege to Grant at Petersburg, guarding Richmond. Desertion intensified as men left the front to save their families and homes from the Yankee invaders.

Sherman delivered the city of Savannah as a Christmas present to Lincoln. The newfound "might" of the Union army gave life to "right" and Congress passed the 13th Amendment to the Constitution. Lincoln met with Confederate representatives to discuss peace. Davis was unimpressed.

December 22, 1864

ANDERSON: About six weeks ago, General William T. Sherman led his 60,000-man army out of Atlanta towards the

eastern seaboard of the Confederacy, leaving his supply line behind, destination unknown.

Before departing, Sherman wrote, "I can make this march and make Georgia howl!" He then cut his communication lines. There has been no news from him since.

Until today, when the President received the following dispatch: "I beg to present you as a

Christmas gift the city of Savannah, with one hundred and fifty heavy guns and plenty of ammunition, also about twenty-five thousand bales of cotton."

We have learned that Sherman's troops marched across Georgia divided into three divisions stretching 60-miles wide. Along the way, they burned and looted plantations and public buildings. Slaves by the thousands left their masters and followed the Union troops to freedom. Neither the Confederacy nor Georgia offered much resistance.

Sherman's march left a wasteland in its wake, destroying major sources of supply for Confederate armies. In doing so, he brought the war home to the populace, endeavoring to break their morale and weaken their will to continue the fight.

Danielle Burke has more on the condition of the Confederacy.

BURKE:

Carter, when Union forces swept through Georgia, essentially at will, the psychological impact on Southerners was as devastating as the impact on the countryside. Yankee soldiers destroyed all sources of food and forage and left behind a hungry and demoralized people. As was their intent, they made the "old and young, rich and poor, feel the hard hand of the war."

ANDERSON: Danielle, what is the sentiment in Richmond?

BURKE: Carter, there are rumblings of dissension among some governors, but President Davis remains as determined as ever to fight to the last.

DAVIS: In a word, peace is impossible without independence, and it is not to be expected that the enemy will anticipate neutrals in the recognition of that independence.

In the hope that the day will soon be reached when, under Divine favor, these States may be allowed to enter on their former peaceful pursuits and to develop the abundant natural resources with which they are blessed, let us, then, resolutely continue to devote our united and unimpaired energies to the defense of our homes, our lives, and our liberties.

This is the true path to peace. Let us tread it with confidence in the assured result.

January 15, 1865

BURKE:
The surrender of Fort Fisher has many Confederate officials convinced that "we cannot carry on the war any longer." The Fort was the only remaining protection for Confederate blockade-runners and the primary defense for the Wilmington supply line that brings food and munitions to General Lee's Army of Northern Virginia, still under siege at Petersburg.

Fort Fisher's fall also left the Confederacy vulnerable to the advancing march of General Sherman's troops as he moves up the coastline to get behind General Lee's Army.

January 31, 1865

CHASE:
Today, the U.S. House of Representatives passed an amendment to abolish slavery. The Senate had previously passed the same amendment on April 8th of last year.

The vote of 119 to 56 narrowly reached the required two-thirds majority. The House exploded into celebration, with some members openly weeping. Black onlookers, who only this year have been allowed to attend Congressional sessions, cheered from the galleries.

Ironically, if ratified by the states, it would displace the Corwin Amendment as the 13th Amendment to the Constitution. The Corwin amendment, pending before the states since March 2, 1861, would shield domestic institutions of the states from the constitutional amendment process and from abolition or interference by Congress.

THE PEACE COMMISSION.
Flying to Abraham's Bosom.

William Lloyd Garrison, who has waged a decades-long fight to end slavery wrote to the President,

"God save you, and bless you abundantly! As an instrument in his hands, you have done a mighty work for the freedom of the millions who have so long pined in bondage in our land – nay, for the freedom of all mankind."

LINCOLN:

I have only been an instrument. The logic and moral power of Garrison and the anti-slavery people of the country and the army have done all. But this amendment is a King's cure for all the evils. It winds the whole thing up. It is the fitting if not indispensable adjunct to the consummation of the great game we are playing.

February 3, 1865

BURKE:

An attempt at peace occurred today on the steamship River Queen, near Union-controlled Fort Monroe in Hampton, Virginia. Vice President Alexander Stephens, Senator Robert Hunter, and Assistant Secretary of War John Campbell met with President Abraham Lincoln and Secretary of State William H. Seward.

LINCOLN:

As to peace, I have said before, and now repeat that three things are indispensable:

The restoration of the national authority throughout the United States.

No receding by the Executive of the United States on the slavery question from the position assumed thereon in the last annual message, and in preceding documents.

No cessation of hostilities short of an end of the war, and the disbanding of all forces hostile to the government.

BURKE:

The disappointed commissioners relayed Lincoln's terms to Jefferson Davis.

DAVIS:

The proposition is insulting. The enemy refuses to enter into negotiations with the Confederate States, or any one of them separately, or to give our people any other terms or guarantees than those which a conqueror may grant or permit us to have peace on any other basis than our unconditional submission to their rule, coupled with the acceptance of their recent legislation, including an amendment to the Constitution for the emancipation of the negro slaves, and with the right, on the part of the Federal Congress, to legislate on the subject of the relations between the white and black populations of each State.

March 1, 1865

ANDERSON:

When General Sherman's forces left Savannah, Georgia on the 30th of January, they headed straight for Columbia, South Carolina, the state capital where the secession movement began.

He said at that time, "The whole army is burning with an insatiable desire to wreak vengeance upon

South Carolina. I almost tremble at her fate, but feel that she deserves all that seems in store for her."

Sherman's warning could not have been more prophetic.

His 65,000-man army covered 10 to 12 miles a day, burning a swath 60 miles wide in grim determination readily viewed as retribution. An abundance of alcohol greeted the Union army as it entered Columbia on February 17. Vengeance fueled by alcohol culminated in the looting and burning of the city, described by a Union war correspondent as "the most monstrous barbarity of the barbarous march."

The next day, Old Glory again flew over Fort Sumter.

Chapter 22 – With Malice toward None

*R**e-elected President Abraham Lincoln delivers a message for the ages with an inaugural address that also hints at how he would welcome the South back into the Union.*

March 4, 1865

ANDERSON: Abraham Lincoln was sworn in today by his former Treasury Secretary and now Chief Justice of the Supreme Court, Salmon P. Chase. He then delivered his second inaugural address which, just 701 words long, took less than seven minutes to deliver.

DOUGLASS: Reaching the Capitol, I took my place in the crowd where I could see the presidential procession as it came upon the east portico, and where I could hear and see all that took place. The whole proceeding was wonderfully quiet, earnest, and solemn. There was a leaden stillness about the crowd. The address sounded more like a sermon than a state paper.

LINCOLN: Fellow-Countrymen:

At this second appearing to take the oath of the Presidential office there is less occasion for an extended address than there was at the first. Then a statement somewhat in detail of a course to be pursued seemed fitting and proper. Now, at the expiration of four years, during which public declarations have been constantly called forth on every point and phase of the great contest which still absorbs the attention and engrosses the energies of the nation, little that is new could be presented.

The progress of our arms, upon which all else chiefly depends, is as well known to the public as to myself, and it is, I trust, reasonably satisfactory and encouraging to all. With high hope for the future, no prediction in regard to it is ventured.

On the occasion corresponding to this four years ago, all thoughts were anxiously directed to an impending civil war. All dreaded it, all sought to avert it. While the inaugural address was being delivered from this place, devoted altogether to saving the Union without war, insurgent agents were in the city seeking to destroy it without war--seeking to dissolve the Union and divide effects by negotiation.

Both parties deprecated war, but one of them would make war rather than let the nation survive, and the other would accept war rather than let it perish, and the war came.

THE AUCTION SALE. *Page 174.*

One-eighth of the whole population were colored slaves, not distributed generally over the Union, but localized in the southern part of it. These slaves constituted a peculiar and powerful interest. All knew that this interest was somehow the cause of the war. To strengthen, perpetuate, and extend this interest was the object for which the insurgents would rend the Union even by war, while the Government claimed no right to do more than to restrict the territorial enlargement of it.

Neither party expected for the war the magnitude or the duration which it has already attained. Neither anticipated that the cause of the conflict might cease with or even before the conflict itself should cease. Each looked for an easier triumph and a result less fundamental and astounding. Both read the same

Bible and pray to the same God, and each invokes His aid against the other.

It may seem strange that any men should dare to ask a just God's assistance in wringing their bread from the sweat of other men's faces, but let us judge not, that we be not judged.

The prayers of both could not be answered. That of neither has been answered fully. The Almighty has His own purposes. "Woe unto the world because of offenses; for it must needs be that offenses come, but woe to that man by whom the offense cometh."

If we shall suppose that American slavery is one of those offenses which, in the providence of God, must needs come, but which, having continued through His appointed time, He now wills to remove, and that He gives to both North and South this terrible war as the woe due to those by whom the offense came, shall we discern therein any departure from those divine attributes which the believers in a living God always ascribe to Him?

Fondly do we hope, fervently do we pray, that this mighty scourge of war may speedily pass away. Yet, if God wills that it continue until all the wealth piled by the bondsman's two hundred and fifty years of unrequited toil shall be sunk, and until every drop of blood drawn with the lash shall be paid by another drawn with the sword, as was said three thousand years ago, so still it must be said "the judgments of the Lord are true and righteous altogether."

With malice toward none, with charity for all, with firmness in the right as God gives us to see the right, let us strive on to finish the work we are in, to bind up the nation's wounds, to care for him who shall have borne the battle and for his widow and his orphan, to do all which may achieve and cherish a just and lasting peace among ourselves and with all nations.

DOUGLASS: For the first time in my life, and I suppose the first time in any colored man's life, I attended the reception of President Lincoln on the evening of the inauguration. As I approached the door, I was

seized by two policemen and forbidden to enter. I said to them that they were mistaken entirely in what they were doing, that if Mr. Lincoln knew that I was at the door he would order my admission, and I bolted in by them.

On the inside, I was taken charge of by two other policemen, to be conducted as I supposed to the President, but instead of that they were conducting me out the window on a plank.

'Oh,' said I, 'this will not do, gentlemen,' and as a gentleman was passing in, I said to him, 'Just say to Mr. Lincoln that Frederick Douglass is at the door.'

He rushed in to President Lincoln, and almost in less than half a minute, I was invited into the East Room of the White House. A perfect sea of beauty and elegance, too, it was. The ladies were in very fine attire, and Mrs. Lincoln was standing there.

I could not have been more than ten feet from him when Mr. Lincoln saw me; his countenance lighted up, and his voice was heard all around.

LINCOLN: Here comes my friend Douglass.

DOUGLASS: As I approached him, he reached out his hand, gave me a cordial shake.

LINCOLN: Douglass, I saw you in the crowd today listening to my inaugural address. There is no man's opinion that I value more than yours; what do you think of it?

DOUGLASS: Mr. Lincoln, I cannot stop here to talk with you, as there are thousands waiting to shake you by the hand.

LINCOLN: What did you think of it?

DOUGLASS: Mr. Lincoln, it was a sacred effort.

Chapter 23 - Appomattox

*W*ith Sheridan on his western flank, Sherman coming up from the South on his rear, and Grant relentlessly pushing the envelope in his front, Lee had no choice but to evacuate his position at Petersburg and leave Richmond unprotected. Lee headed west, the Confederate government headed south and Lincoln went to Richmond.

Lee was expecting to find rations at Appomattox and an escape route. Sheridan beat him there and seized his rations. Lee met with Grant to discuss terms while Lincoln returned to Washington.

Amid the jubilation and celebrations, Lincoln, rather informally from the second floor of the White House, asked the crowd to look forward to the next task at hand - reconstruction - and to accept Louisiana as a model for Southern states to rejoin the Union. For the first time publicly, Lincoln expressed support to the idea of enfranchising former slaves. In the crowd was a famous and firm supporter of the Confederate cause - John Wilkes Booth. Booth is quoted as saying upon hearing Lincoln's words: "That means nigger citizenship. Now, by God, I'll put him through. That is the last speech he will ever give."

April 3, 1865

ANDERSON: With General Sherman's army closing in from the south, General Ulysses S. Grant began his offensive against the Confederate Army of Northern Virginia defending Petersburg and Richmond by sending the Union cavalry under General Sheridan to secure the South Side Railroad, the last rail line into Petersburg.

On the 1st of April, at a country crossroads in Dinwiddie County known as Five Forks, 12 miles west of Petersburg, Sheridan defeated a Confederate force led by General George Pickett, capturing artillery and many prisoners.

After nine and a half months of fighting in the trenches around Petersburg, characterized by infantry and artillery behind the protection of defenses, it took the Union Cavalry charging across an open landscape to break the siege.

CHASE: At the beginning of the war, the US Army could barely muster a cavalry at all, enabling the Rebel cavalry to move about the landscape almost at will.

Today, the Army of the Potomac's Cavalry Corps is a magnificent fighting force of 10,000 horse and horsemen, sharply attired in blue uniform and gold piping, equipped with rapid-fire carbines. They faced a ragged enemy, many without overcoats or blankets, clad in tattered remnants of Jacket and Pantaloons.

ANDERSON: General Lee directed Pickett to "hold Five Forks at all hazards," sending three brigades from the forces defending Petersburg for support. When Grant learned that Lee had weakened his defenses, he ordered a general assault.

At midnight, Union guns opened fire on the Confederate fortifications. In the ten months that Lee's army had held the line at Petersburg, they had endured many bombardments, but nothing like this one. The night sky was filled with the burning arcs of shells as they made their way towards the Confederate line.

At dawn, the Union infantry attacked the weakened defenses of Petersburg.

BURKE: This is Danielle Burke in Richmond.

When the Confederate line was breached, General Lee telegraphed

Richmond that it was necessary he abandon his position that night or run the risk of being cut off in the morning. He advised the Government to make all preparation for evacuating Richmond immediately.

Being Sunday, President Davis was sitting in his usual pew in St. Paul's Episcopal Church when the messenger strode up the aisle and handed him a telegram. Davis read it silently, then arose and walked quietly out of the church.

The Confederate Cabinet met and decided to move the Government to Danville. All afternoon, documents and records were hastily packed. The Confederate treasury, $500,000 in gold and silver, went at once by special train, guarded by sixty naval cadets. The Presidential train followed.

CHASE: This is Jackie Chase in Richmond, Virginia.

At daybreak this morning, Federal troops entered the abandoned Confederate capital.

From the moment Union troops entered the city, blacks of Richmond jammed the sidewalks to catch a glimpse of the spectacle. No longer enslaved, they thrust out their hands to be shaken by soldiers, and presented them with offerings of fruit, flowers, even jugs of whiskey. To the sounds of 'John Brown's Body,' they danced with unimpeded joy.

The capture of Richmond has been the goal of the Union Army since the beginning of the War. The Confederate capital lay tantalizingly close to Washington - only 100 miles away - but it took four years of hard fighting and unspeakable bloodshed to get here.

April 5, 1865

ANDERSON: Upon hearing the news of the fall of Richmond, President Lincoln accompanied by his son Tad, set sail for the Confederate capital aboard the River Queen.

LINCOLN: Thank God that I have lived to see this! It seems to me that I have been dreaming a horrid dream for four years, and now the nightmare is gone. I want to see Richmond.

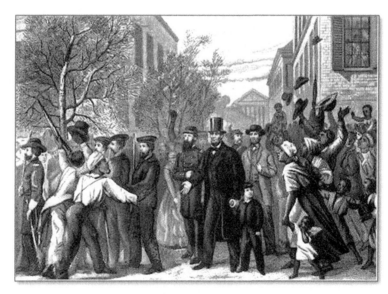

CHASE: Negroes shouted that the President had arrived. Thinking the news was about Jefferson Davis, they cried 'Hang him!' 'Hang him!' 'Show him no quarter!'. But when they learned it was President Lincoln, dozens of them raced to the landing, yelling and screaming "Hallelujah!" and "Glory! President Lincoln has come!"

Hearing the commotion, more blacks – men, women, and children – poured into the streets. An old man sprang forward. 'Bless the Lord. There is the great Messiah!' And he fell upon his knees before the President. The others followed his example, and in a minute, a throng of kneeling men, women and children surrounded Mr. Lincoln.

LINCOLN: Don't kneel to me. That is not right. You must kneel to God only, and thank him for the liberty you will hereafter enjoy. I am but God's humble instrument; but you may rest assured that as long as I live no one shall put a shackle on your limbs, and you shall have all the rights which God has given to every other free citizen of this Republic.

CHASE: Soon the President was walking through streets alive with spectators. There is no describing the scene along the route. The colored population was wild with enthusiasm. Old men thanked God in a very boisterous manner, and old women shouted as high as they had ever done at religious revival.

Before departing the city, the President noticed three recently orphaned kittens which were mewing piteously. He picked them up, took them on his lap and stroked them.

LINCOLN: Poor little creatures, don't cry; you'll be taken good care of.   Colonel, see that these poor little motherless waifs are given plenty of milk and treated kindly.

CHASE: To all who witnessed this expression of tenderness, it was a most extraordinary experience. After the horrors of the war, the enormous loss of life and limb, the many rivers of blood, here was the man who signed the commissions of all the heroic men who served the cause of the Union openly revealing a most generous spirit. Perhaps this is his way of saying it is now time for compassion and forgiveness.

DAVIS: We have now entered upon a new phase of a struggle the memory of which is to endure for all ages and to shed an increasing luster upon our country.

Relieved from the necessity of guarding cities and particular points, with an army operating on the interior of our own country, nothing is now needed to render our triumph certain but the exhibition of our own unquenchable resolve.

Animated by the confidence in your spirit and fortitude, which never yet has failed me, I announce to you, fellow-countrymen, that it is my purpose to maintain your cause with my whole heart and soul; that I will never consent to abandon to the enemy one foot of the soil of any one of the States of the Confederacy.

Let us not, then, despond, my countrymen; but, relying on the never-failing mercies and protecting care of our God, let us meet the foe with fresh defiance, with unconquered and unconquerable hearts.

April 7, 1865

ANDERSON: The Confederate Army of Northern Virginia is racing against hunger and time as they seek to escape the Union Army's capture of Petersburg and Richmond. General Lee sent a telegraph down the railroad line for 200,000 rations to be sent ahead. Their only hope now is to outdistance

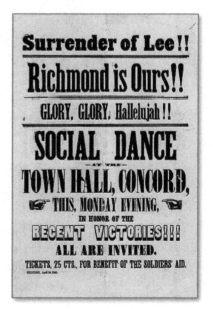

the Federals in a race to Appomattox Station and badly needed rations.

CHASE:
Carter, General Sheridan got to Appomattox Court House first and placed his immense cavalry corps between Appomattox Station and the Court House, directly across the path of Lee's retreat. A unit under command of the young General George Armstrong Custer took control of the Jetersville station and intercepted the trains carrying Confederate rations. There are no rations on their way to Appomattox.

April 8, 1865

BURKE:
The splendid Army of Northern Virginia, which quickly became the envy of the world for its courage, heroism and achievement, has been reduced to a fragment of brave men, many of whom, from exposure and want of food, cannot lift a musket to the shoulder. Desertions have intensified with each passing hour.

At 8:30 this morning, General Robert E. Lee could no longer put off the inevitable. He ordered

General Longstreet to stop fighting and commenced riding toward the Union front to make arrangements to see General Grant.

When General Grant finally heard the news, he sent one of his aides forward to arrange a suitable place for the surrender. The Courthouse itself was the most likely place in the village, but, being Sunday, was not open. The Wilmer McLean house, just a few hundred yards away and the most prominent residence in the small village, was then selected.

April 9, 1865

CHASE: General Lee arrived at the McLean house first and sat in a large sitting room on the first floor. At about one o'clock, General Grant and his staff arrived. Grant sat at a marble-topped table in the center of the room, Lee at a small oval table near the front window.

General Grant, not yet forty-three years old, five feet eight inches tall, shoulders slightly stooped, was clothed in a uniform that included no marks of rank except a general's shoulder straps.

BURKE: General Lee, fifty-eight years old, six feet tall, hair and beard silver gray, wore a handsome uniform of Confederate gray buttoned to the throat, with three stars on each side of the turned-down collar, and a splendid sword at his side.

ANDERSON: The formalities were concluded without dramatic accessories. Grant did not demand Lee's sword, as is customary, but actually apologized to him for not having his own, saying it had been left behind in the wagon. He also did not allow the firing of salutes by Union soldiers to mark the event.

Grant asked only that the officers and men of the Army of Northern Virginia surrender and give their word not to take up arms against the United States until properly exchanged. Lee accepted the terms.

Lieutenant Colonel Ely Parker quietly transcribed the final copy before the two generals scrawled their names.

Lee then conveyed to Grant that his men have been living for the last few days principally upon parched corn and are thereby badly in need of rations and forage. Grant responded that he would send twenty five thousand rations.

Lee, ever courteous, shook each man's hand. When he got to Colonel Parker, a Seneca Indian, Lee hesitated, and then extending his hand to Parker said, 'I am glad to see one real American here.' Parker accepted the proffered handshake, responding, '"We are all Americans.'"

Lee went out to the front porch of the McLean house, mounted his horse, Traveler, and raised his hat in salute as he rode back to his lines. The Union soldiers presented arms in a dramatic show of respect to the soldier and the man.

General Lee said to all, "Let us go home and cultivate our virtues."

April 11, 1865

CHASE: This is Jackie Chase in Washington, DC which is still celebrating the news that Confederate General Robert E. Lee had surrendered to General Grant at Appomattox. A jubilant crowd has gathered outside the White House calling for President Lincoln.

Lincoln stood at the window over the building's main door, a place where presidents customarily gave speeches. A reporter held a light so Lincoln could read his speech, while young Tad Lincoln grasped the pages as they fluttered to his feet.

For the first time in a public speech, Lincoln expressed his support for black suffrage.

LINCOLN: The evacuation of Petersburg and Richmond, and the surrender of the principal insurgent army, give hope of a righteous and speedy peace whose joyous expression cannot be restrained. In the midst of this, however, He, from Whom all blessings flow, must not be forgotten.

Chapter 24 – Eulogy

DOUGLASS:

The name of Abraham Lincoln was near and dear to our hearts in the darkest and most perilous hours of the Republic.

Despite the mist and haze that surrounded him; despite the tumult, the hurry, and confusion of the hour, we came to the conclusion that the hour and the man of our redemption had somehow met in the person of Abraham Lincoln.

Few great public men have ever been the victims of fiercer denunciation than Abraham Lincoln was during his administration. He was often wounded in the house of his friends. Reproaches came thick and fast upon him from within and from without, and from opposite quarters.

He was assailed by Abolitionists; he was assailed by slaveholders; he was assailed by the men who were for peace at any price; he was assailed, by those who were for a more vigorous prosecution of the war; he was assailed for not making the war an abolition war; and he was bitterly assailed for making the war an abolition war.

The judgment of the present hour is that measuring the tremendous magnitude of the work before him, infinite wisdom has seldom sent any man into the world better fitted for his mission than Abraham Lincoln.

The tremendous question for him to decide was whether his country should survive the crisis and flourish, or be dismembered and perish.

He brought his strong common sense, sharpened in the school of adversity, to bear upon the question. He did not hesitate, he did not doubt, he did not falter; but at once resolved that at whatever peril, at whatever cost, the union of the States should be preserved.

He calmly and bravely heard the voice of doubt and fear all around him; but he had an oath in heaven, and there was not power enough on earth to make this honest boatman, backwoodsman, and broad-handed splitter of rails evade or violate that sacred oath.

Fellow citizens, the fourteenth day of April 1865 is now and will ever remain a memorable day in the annals of this Republic. It was on the evening of this day, while a fierce and sanguinary rebellion was in the last stages of its desolating power; while its armies were broken and scattered before the invincible armies of Grant and Sherman; while a great nation, torn and rent by war, was already beginning to raise to the skies loud anthems of joy at the dawn of peace, it was startled, amazed, and overwhelmed by the crowning crime of slavery — the assassination of Abraham Lincoln.

It was a new crime, a pure act of malice. No purpose of the rebellion was to be served by it. It was the simple gratification of a hell-black spirit of revenge.

But it has done good after all. It has filled the country with a deeper abhorrence of slavery and a deeper love for the great liberator.

Had Abraham Lincoln died from any of the numerous ills to which flesh is heir; had he reached that good old age of which his vigorous constitution and his temperate habits gave promise; had he been permitted to see the end of his great work; had the solemn curtain of death come down but gradually — we should still have been smitten with a heavy grief, and treasured his name lovingly.

But dying as he did die, by the red hand of violence, killed, assassinated, taken off without warning, not because of personal hate — for no man who knew Abraham Lincoln could hate him — but because of his fidelity to union and liberty, he is doubly dear to us, and his memory will be precious forever.

Epilogue

A few days later, on April 14, Good Friday, Booth carried out his threat by shooting Abraham Lincoln while he attended the play, *Our American Cousin,* at Ford's Theatre. The President died the next day.

That day, General Robert Anderson, who surrendered Fort Sumter on April 12, 1861, raised the Stars and Stripes over Fort Sumter, assisted by none other than Frederick Douglass.

Lincoln's open coffin lay in state at the White House on the 18th and was then moved to the U.S. Capitol rotunda on the 21st.

After public viewing in Washington, DC, Lincoln's coffin was placed on a funeral train, along with the remains of his son Willie, headed for his final resting place in Springfield, Illinois.

The route followed the one taken by president-elect Lincoln when he departed his hometown for his inauguration as the 16th President. The trip covered 1,654 miles through 180 cities and seven states to allow the Northern public an opportunity to pay their last respects.

News of Lee's surrender slowly made its way to Johnston and Sherman in North Carolina. On April 17, the two commanders met in Durham Station, North Carolina, to discuss terms. At first, Sherman offered more generous terms than were offered by Grant to Lee. Secretary of War Edwin Stanton, embittered by Lincoln's murder, refused to approve the terms. On April 26, Johnston surrendered his 37,000 men on the same conditions as those given to Lee at Appomattox Court House.

Only two sizable Confederate armies remained. One was in Louisiana, led by General Richard Taylor, brother-in-law of Jefferson Davis and son of President Zachary Taylor. He surrendered on May 4.

The other army was in Texas and commanded by General Edmund Kirby Smith. Smith surrendered on May 26.

On May 10, Jefferson Davis was captured in Georgia and immediately imprisoned.

The last battle of the Civil War occurred in Cameron County, Texas on May 12 to May 14. Native, African, and Hispanic Americans were all involved in the fighting. The Confederates won.

Not all parts of the country learned of the war's end and slavery's abolition. In Texas, it was not until June 19th when Major General Gordon Granger landed at Galveston, Texas with news that the war had ended were slaves set free. Juneteenth is celebrated to this day.

The last Confederate surrender occurred in Liverpool when the Confederate warship CSS Shenandoah arrived there on November 7, 1865. The Shenandoah was also responsible for firing the last shot of the American Civil War at a whaler off the Aleutian Islands in June 1865.

The ship's Captain was unaware of the Confederate surrender and continued to sink Union merchant ships off Alaska, until he learned the news while in San Francisco harbor on August 2nd. He immediately set sail for Liverpool in fear of being tried as pirates in the U.S. The terms of the Confederate surrender did not extend amnesty to Confederate sailors, only its soldiers.

On December 6, 1865, the Georgia legislature ratified the 13th Amendment to the Constitution, becoming the 27th state out of 36 to do so, thereby meeting the three-fourths requirement of the Constitution. Secretary of State Seward, on December 18, 1865, certified that the Thirteenth Amendment had become valid, "to all intents and purposes, as a part of the Constitution."

Oregon, California, Florida and Iowa quickly followed suit. Delaware and New Jersey were the only Northern states to reject the amendment. New Jersey finally ratified it in 1866. Delaware did so in 1901.

Kentucky did not ratify it until 1976; Mississippi did not do so until 1995.

In 1873, the United States Government demanded the British Government pay compensation for the damage caused by Confederate ships during the war. The British allowed the Confederate government to purchase ships built in England and dock in British ports. It became known as the 'Alabama Claim' because the Alabama had caused the most damage. The British Government paid £3,000,000.

The approximately 10,455 military engagements plus naval clashes, accidents, suicides, sicknesses, murders and executions resulted in total civilian and military casualties of 1,094,453 during the Civil War.

Ten percent of all Northern men aged 20-45 died, along with 30 percent of all Southern white males aged 18-40. It has been estimated that over 1 million horses were killed during the war.

In 1879, the Civil War was estimated by Congress to have cost approximately $10 billion, not including the cost of soldier pensions. Adjusting that for inflation and population difference, it would yield a 2015 equivalent of $2.4 trillion.

Image Credits

1. Cover: Sergeant A.M. Chandler of the 44th Mississippi Infantry Regiment, Co. F., and Silas Chandler, family slave, with Bowie knives, revolvers, pepper-box, shotgun, and canteen. (Library of Congress.)

2. Prologue: Henry David Thoreau, Courtesy of Concord Free Public Library.

3. Prologue: Frederick Douglass, 1866. By the time this photograph of Frederick Douglass was taken, slavery in the United States had been abolished. After the Civil War Douglass would to fight for the rights of blacks, as well as for women. In 1889 he was appointed U.S. minister to Haiti. Collection of the New York Historical Society.

4. Prologue: Abolitionist John Brown in a c.1847 daguerreotype taken by Augustus Washington, National Portrait Gallery.

5. Chapter 1:   "Lincoln Elected" Front page of a Republican newspaper celebrates Lincoln's election. Lincoln swept every free northern state except New Jersey for a total of 180 electoral votes but garnered not one electoral vote in the southern and border states, whose vote was split between John Breckinridge and John Bell. With a turnout of 81.2% as backdrop, Lincoln captured only 39.8% of the popular vote while his debate rival, Stephen A. Douglas got 29.5% of the popular vote but only one electoral vote.

6. Chapter 1:   "The Two Platforms" Democratic Party poster, June 18, 1860. The sixth resolution confirmed the Party's support for slavery, read as follows: "That the enactments of the State Legislatures to defeat the faithful execution of the Fugitive Slave Law, are hostile in character, subversive of the Constitution, and revolutionary in their effect."

7. Chapter 1:   "The United States—A Black business." This political cartoon depicts two Americans—a northerner and a southerner—standing on opposite sides of a black male slave. The slave is holding a map of the United States, tearing it in half along the North-South border. Published November 8, 1856 in *Punch*, years

before the outbreak of Civil War in the United States, the cartoon demonstrates the English understanding of 'The Negro Question' and its repercussions for the American states. The image shows a black slave at the middle of the conflict between North and South, standing between the Southern farmer and the Yankee gentleman as he tears a map of America in a symbolic gesture that literally rips the nation's fabric in two. (Library of Congress)

8.   Chapter 1:   "Little Bo-Peep and her foolish sheep." The second in a series of caricatures criticizing the secession of several Southern states from the Union during the last months of the Buchanan administration. Here the young nursery-rhyme shepherdess Bo-Peep represents the Union. She stands at left wearing a dress of stars-and-stripes bunting and with an eagle beside her, watching as seven of her sheep flee into a forest of palmetto trees infested with wolves. (The palmetto is the symbol of South Carolina, the leading secessionist state and first to dissolve ties with the United States.) The wolves wear crowns and represent the European powers which some feared would prey on the newly independent states. They prowl about and say, "If we can only get them separated from the flock, we can pick their bones at our leisure." Back in the clearing, grazing about Bo-Peep, are the remaining flock, two of which are labeled Virginia (closest to her) and Kansas. An old dog "Hickory" lies dead in the grass while another, named "Old Buck," flees toward the left. B o-Peep vainly calls, "Sic 'em Buck! sic 'em! I wish poor old Hickory was alive. He'd bring 'em back in no time." Buck is lame duck president James Buchanan, who proved ineffectual against the secessionist threat to the Union. "Old Hickory" was the nickname of former Democratic president Andrew Jackson, venerated as a champion of a strong federal union. Although unsigned, the print seems on stylistic grounds to have been drawn by John H. Goater, the artist responsible for numbers one, three, and probably four in the "Dime Caricatures" series. (Library of Congress)

9.   Chapter 1:   "The outbreak of the rebellion in the United States 1861." Published by Kimmel & Forster, 254 & 265 Canal St, New York, c1865. A grand allegory of the Civil War in America, harshly critical of the Buchanan administration, Jefferson Davis, and the Confederacy. In the center stands Liberty, wearing a Phrygian cap and a laurel wreath. She is flanked by the figures of Justice (holding a sword and scales) and Abraham Lincoln. Principal figures (from left to right) are: Confederate president Jefferson Davis (beneath a

palm tree about whose trunk winds a poisonous snake), James Buchanan (asleep), his secretary of war John B. Floyd, who was accused of misappropriation of government funds (raking coins into a bag), Justice, Columbia, Lincoln, Gen. Winfield Scott (in military uniform), and various figures exemplifying the generosity and suffering of the Northern citizenry. The left foreground is filled with Confederate soldiers, some of them engaged in tearing the Union flag from the hands of other soldiers. In the background are scenes of war. In contrast, on the right, the sun rises over mountains in the distance beyond a prosperous countryside. (Library of Congress)

10. Chapter 2: "The Union Is Dissolved!" Printed in Charleston, South Carolina, on December 20, 1860, this broadside announces South Carolina's repeal of the Constitution of the United States and the state's secession from the Union. *Charleston Mercury,* December 20, 1860. (American Treasures of the Library of Congress)

11. Chapter 2: Photograph of Lincoln's Springfield Home. Lincoln can be seen with his sons, Willie and Tad, taken during the summer of 1860 by John Adams Whipple. (National Park Service)

12. Chapter 2: Major Robert Anderson, c. 1861, Federal commander of Fort Sumter at the beginning of the war, surrendered the fort to the Confederacy after 34 hours of bombardment. (Library of Congress)

13. Chapter 2: One of three similar prints published by Oliver Evans Woods, reflecting grave northern fears of British and French interference on behalf of the Confederacy in the Civil War. (See also "The Pending Conflict" and "The Pending Contest," nos. 1864-2 and 1864-3.) The controversy centered on the "Alabama" and other warships built and fitted out for the Confederates in England. French Emperor Napoleon III's military operations in Mexico in 1862 and 1863 were also perceived as dangerous to the North. The print actually appeared in the summer of 1863, when Southern diplomatic overtures to France and England threatened to result in international recognition for the Confederacy. In the center Jefferson Davis--here called "Secesh"--raises a club labeled "Pirate Alabama" over the head of a brawny Union soldier whose arms are constricted by the Constitution, and around whose waist and legs coils a poisonous snake. Davis tramples on an American flag. At right stands a leering

John Bull, who holds a pile of clubs in reserve for Davis. Behind him is a prancing Napoleon III, also watching the contest. Soldier: "The flag of my country trampled underfoot--the ships of my country burning on the ocean--while I stand here entangled in the coils of this foul Copperhead, and so bound up by Constitutional restraints, that I am unable to put forth my true strength in their behalf." The "restraints" mentioned may refer to opposition on constitutional grounds to Lincoln's use of what he considered valid presidential war powers. The cartoon may have been specifically occasioned by the Supreme Court's review in the "Prize Cases" of 1863 of the legality of the Union blockade. "Copperhead" was the derogatory term used for anti-Lincoln or anti-Republican advocates of a negotiated reconciliation with the South. (Library of Congress)

14.   Chapter 2:   Abraham Lincoln by Alexander Hesler, Springfield, Illinois. One of three photographs taken by Hesler during a sitting on June 3, 1860 while Lincoln was campaigning for the presidency. Of these portraits Lincoln said, "That looks better and expresses me better than any I have ever seen; if it pleases the people I am satisfied." This print was made late in the nineteenth century by George B. Ayres. The negative for this image survives in the Smithsonian Institution, although it is now shattered.

15.   Chapter 2:   Jefferson Davis by Matthew Brady. Albumen silver print (*carte de visite*), 1861, National Portrait Gallery, Smithsonian Institution.

16.   Chapter 3:   "Our national bird as it appeared when handed to James Buchanan, March 4, 1857. The identical bird as it appeared A. D. 1861." The iconic national bird, representing the Union, is strong and healthy at the beginning of Democrat James Buchanan's administration. By the time Republican Abraham Lincoln assumed the Presidency, it is gaunt and emaciated reflecting the secession of 11 southern states from the Union. This political cartoon highlights the rising tensions over states' rights during the antebellum period and the ultimate dissolution of the Union in 1861. The fact that Buchanan's administration was riddled with corruption and charges of bribery and graft, only worsened the toll that years fighting over slavery and states' rights had taken on the nation's vitality. Artist: Woolf, Michael Angelo, 1837-1899. (Boston Public Library, Print Department)

17. Chapter 3: This leaf features an illustration of the Inauguration of Abraham Lincoln by Winslow Homer from the original March 16, 1861 edition of *Harper's Weekly*. Mr. Lincoln is pictured giving his Inaugural address on the steps of the U.S. Capitol. From a drawing made on the spot. (Winslow Homer Collection, Boston Public Library, Print Department).

18. Chapter 3: "Bombardment of Fort Sumter by the batteries of the Confederate states." On April 12, 1861, Confederate forces opened fire on Fort Sumter, the nearly completed federal garrison positioned on a man-made island in South Carolina's Charleston harbor. In his inaugural address, Lincoln committed "to hold, occupy, and possess the property and places belonging to the Government" without provoking violence. Fort Sumter qualified as property of the federal government, but occupying it and supplying its occupants was the subject of intense debate within Lincoln's cabinet. The Union was not ready for war. While the North was industrially superior and vastly more populous than the South, the majority of the nation's soldiers and military brain power resided in Confederate states. The President dispatched a messenger on April 6 to inform the Confederate leadership of intentions to supply Fort Sumter with "provisions, only". On April 9, Davis and his cabinet, convinced that an attack on Sumter would sway the unaffiliated upper South to their cause, resolved to take the fort before it could be resupplied. Robert Toombs, serving as Confederate secretary of state, warned President Davis that firing on Fort Sumter "will inaugurate a civil war greater than any the world has yet seen. ... It is suicide, murder, and will lose us every friend at the North. You will wantonly strike a hornet's nest which extends from mountains to ocean, and legions now quiet will storm out and sting us to death. It is unnecessary; it puts us in the wrong; it is fatal." (Illus. in: *Harper's Weekly*, 1861 April 27, pp. 264-265. (Library of Congress)

19. Chapter 3: "TO ARMS" Poster by John N. Ingersoll, 1861.

20. Chapter 3: Slaves preparing cotton for the cotton gin on a plantation near Beaufort, S.C., 1862. (Library of Congress)

21. Chapter 3: "Scott's Great Snake." This 1861 cartoon propaganda map published in Cincinnati and the patriotic envelope below depict Union general-in-chief Winfield Scott's (1786–1866) plan to crush the South both economically and militarily. Scott's plan

called for a strong blockade of the Southern ports and a major offensive down the Mississippi River to divide the Confederacy and cut off supplies and assistance to its heartland. The press ridiculed Scott's strategy as the "Anaconda Plan," after the snake that kills by constriction, but it had its supporters as the anti-Confederacy envelope illustrates. This general strategy contributed greatly to the eventual Northern victory. J.B. Elliott. Cincinnati: 1861. (Library of Congress)

22. Chapter 3: "Secession Exploded." This strongly anti-Confederate satire is a fantastical vision of the Union defeat of the secessionist movement. A hideous monster representing secession emerges from the water at left. He is hit by a charge from a mammoth cannon "Death to Traitors!" operated by Uncle Sam (right). A two-faced figure representing Baltimore, whose allegiance to the Union was at least questionable during the war, pulls at Uncle Sam's coattails. The explosion sends several small demons, representing the secessionist states, hurling through the air. Prominent among them is South Carolina, in a coffin at upper right. Tennessee and Kentucky, two Southern states internally divided over the secession question, are represented by two-headed creatures. Virginia, though part of the Confederacy, is also shown divided--probably an acknowledgment of the Appalachian and eastern regions' alignment with the Union. Among the demons is a small figure of Tennessee senator and 1860 presidential candidate John Bell, with a bell-shaped body. In the foreground is a large American flag on which Winfield Scott, commander of the Union forces, and a bald eagle rest. (Library of Congress)

23. Chapter 3: A slave family on the auction block in front of perspective slave-buyers. (University of Virginia, Slave Trade Collection)

24. Chapter 4: Mass meeting April 20, 1861, to support the Government at Washington's equestrian statue in New York City. (National Park Service)

25. Chapter 4: Constitution of the Confederate States of America. (University of Georgia Special Collections Libraries)

26. Chapter 4: "Battle at Bull Run." *Louisville Daily Courier,* Kentucky, July 20, 1861.

27. Chapter 4: "Charge of the Black Horse Cavalry upon the Fire Zouaves at the battle of Bull Run." Wood engraving in *Harper's Weekly*, Aug. 10, 1861. (Library of Congress)

28. Chapter 4: "Carrying the wounded at Bull Run." *Harper's Weekly*, August 10, 1861. (Library of Congress)

29. Chapter 4: Major General George B. McClellan, 1861. *Carte-de-visite* photograph by Matthew Brady. (Library of Congress)

30. Chapter 5: General Grant as photographed by Mathew Brady in Cold Harbor, Virginia, in June 1864. (Library of Congress)

31. Chapter 5: "Battle of Pittsburgh Landing, April 7, 1862 – Final and victorious charge of Union Troops under Major General Grant." *Harper's Weekly*. (Library of Congress)

32. Chapter 5: "War News. VICTORY!! New Orleans Taken." The capture of New Orleans began on April 25, 1862, when Flag Officer David G. Farragut asked for the surrender of the city, which was denied. Farragut then moved upriver to subdue the fortifications at Forts Jackson and Saint Philip north of the city. On April 29, Farragut and 250 marines returned and were unopposed in the capture of the city itself. The capture of the Confederates' largest city, an immense strategic and commercial prize, was a turning point in the War.

33. Chapter 5: Robert Knox Sneden's Plan of Fort Magruder. Battlefield of Williamsburg. Sketched the day after the battle, May 6, 1862. (Library of Congress)

34. Chapter 5: View of Vicksburg, Mississippi, 1855. Engraving published August 1855 in Ballou's Pictorial Drawing-Room Companion, Boston, Massachusetts.

35. Chapter 6: Julian Vannerson's photograph of Robert E. Lee in March 1864. (Library of Congress)

36. Chapter 6: Fortifications and the large Parrott guns at Yorktown, during the Peninsula Campaign 1862. James F. Gibson, photographer.

37.   Chapter 6:   "Omaha City, July 4, 1862, Pacific Railroad Bill." The news of the July 1, 1862, Pacific Railroad Act was announced in the July 4 issue of the *Tri-Weekly Republican* in Omaha, Nebraska.

38.   Chapter 6:   The controversial General Benjamin Franklin Butler declares that slaves are "contraband of war" during the Civil War. Charles Carleton Coffin Drum-Beat of the Nation, New York, NY: (Harper & Brothers, 1915)

39.   Chapter 6:   Confederate troops marching west on East Patrick Street, Frederick, Maryland, September 12, 1862.   (Historical Society of Frederick County, Maryland)

40.   Chapter 6:   Photo of Frederick Douglass by unidentified photographer. (National Portrait Gallery, Smithsonian Institution)

41.   Chapter 7:   "The Prayer of Twenty Million." Open letter from Horace Greeley to Abraham Lincoln, August 1, 1862. (Abraham Lincoln Papers at the Library of Congress, Manuscript Division)

42.   Chapter 7:   Poster of slave auction, Cape Girardeau County, Missouri, August 23, 1855.

43.   Chapter 7:   "Am I Not a Man and a Brother?" Design of the medallion created as part of anti-slavery campaign by Joseph Wedgwood, 1787.

44.   Chapter 8:   Dead Confederate soldiers from Sharpe's Louisiana Brigade on the Hagerstown Turnpike, north of the Dunker Church, photographed by Alexander Gardner. (Library of Congress)

45.   Chapter 8:   Several dead soldiers lying outside of Dunker Church, which survived the Battle of Antietam and was used as an aid station, September, 1862, photographed by Alexander Gardner. (Library of Congress)

46.   Chapter 8:   President Abraham Lincoln visiting with Maj. Gen. George McClellan shortly after the Battle of Antietam. (Library of Congress)

47.   Chapter 8:   "The battle of Antietam. The One Hundred and Thirtieth Pennsylvania Regiment of Volunteers burying the Confederate dead, Friday, September 19th, 1862. This spot was the

scene of one of the most desperate conflicts of the war. This scene of the burial of the dead by the One Hundred and Thirtieth Pennsylvania Volunteers is a most interesting part of Antietam battlefield, it being the post where one of the most murderous conflicts took place. The ditch shown in the sketch at nearly right angles was used by the Confederates as a rifle-pit, and from its shelter many a destructive volley was poured upon the Federals. After much maneuvering, the Irish Brigade managed to get on a slight elevation, which commanded a portion of the ditch, while the One Hundred and Thirtieth Pennsylvania Regiment took up another. The Confederates, finding themselves between two fires, retreated, but not till they had lost many men. The next day, when the One Hundred and Thirtieth Regiment was detailed to bury the dead, it found one hundred and thirty-eight dead Confederates in this ditch, a proof of the desperate tenacity with which the position had been defended."– Frank Leslie, 1896. *Frank Leslie Famous Leaders and Battle Scenes of the Civil War,* (New York, NY: Mrs. Frank Leslie, 1896)

48. Chapter 9: "Notice of the Emancipation Proclamation" from *The Alleghenian,* September 25, 1862. (Library of Congress)

49. Chapter 9: "The Great Negro Emancipation." This cartoon was published after the Emancipation Proclamation was announced, but before it took effect. It criticizes Lincoln's emancipation policies by poking fun at his previous advocacy of gradual emancipation and anticipating that he will turn the Emancipation Proclamation into a plan for (very) gradual emancipation. The cartoon manifests the fears of some that the president would not carry out the new policy. The figure viewed from the back, reading the poster, is Horace Greeley ("HG N York"). (*Harper's Weekly,* December 20, 1862)

50. Chapter 9: The first reading of the Emancipation Proclamation before the cabinet / painted by F.B. Carpenter; engraved by A.H. Ritchie, c1866. Print shows a reenactment of Abraham Lincoln signing the Emancipation Proclamation on July 22, 1862, painted by Francis B. Carpenter at the White House in 1864. Depicted, from left to right are: Edwin M. Stanton, Secretary of War, Salmon P. Chase, Secretary of the Treasury, President Lincoln, Gideon Welles, Secretary of the Navy, Caleb B. Smith, Secretary of the Interior, William H. Seward, Secretary of State, Montgomery Blair, Postmaster General, and Edward Bates, Attorney General. Simon

Cameron and Andrew Jackson are featured as paintings. (Library of Congress)

51.   Chapter 10:   "Abe Lincoln's Last Card" was a political cartoon by the Englishman John Tenniel, printed in the *London Times* on October 18, 1862.

52.   Chapter 10:   "Election Of 1862 – Huge Republican Losses!" November 4, 1862. For the Federal government, the war wasn't exactly going well. True, there were some victories in the West, but the failure of campaign after campaign in the East far overshadowed them. Just how much the public took notice and just where they placed the blame became clear on this day. (New York Public Library)

53.   Chapter 10:   "Emancipation of the Negroes, January 1863--the Past and The Future." Drawing by Thomas Nast. *Harper's Weekly,* January 24, 1863. (Library of Congress)

54.   Chapter 11:   In response to Lincoln's concern about the slow pace of the Union troops under General George McClellan, the general responded "You may find those who will go faster than I, Mr. President; but it is very doubtful if you will find many who will go further." Mary Todd Lincoln, who believed her great antipathy to the general was shared by the public, advised her husband in this letter to remove McClellan from the command. Whether she influenced her husband's decision is unknown, but on November 5, 1862, Lincoln placed the Union forces under the command of General Burnside. Holograph, November 2, 1862. Gift of Robert Todd Lincoln, 1923. (Manuscript Division, Library of Congress)

55.   Chapter 11:   "Major General George B. McClellan and staff." Portrait shows from left: Lieut. Williams, A.D.C., Surg. Walters, Brig. Gen. G. W. Morell, Lt. Col. A. V. Colburn, A.D.C., Maj. Gen. G. B. McClellan, Lt. Col. N. B. Switzer, Prince de Joinville, Comte de Paris as identified on the card mount. Photographed March 1862. (Library of Congress)

56.   Chapter 11:   "Our Soldiers in the streets of Fredericksburg." Drawn by A. R. Waud. *Harper's Weekly,* January 3, 1863. (Library of Congress)

57. Chapter 11:   Nathan Kimball's Brigade was the first to attack Marye's Heights.   Disregarding the fire of Confederate guns, Kimball's men advanced steadily to within 60 yards of the stone wall. They could go no further. (Anne S. K. Brown Military Collection, Brow University)

58. Chapter 11:   "The Attack on Fredericksburg-The Forlorn Hope Scaling the Hill." *Harper's Weekly,* December 27, 1862. (Library of Congress)

59. Chapter 11:   Dead at Marye's Heights photographed by Matthew Brady. By the time the Union army crossed the Rappahannock River and entered Fredericksburg, General Lee's army was entrenched 600 yards west of the city on Marye's Heights, which was protected at the base by a stone wall and a sunken road. In the Battle for the Sunken Road, on 13 December 1862, the Union forces suffered severe casualties and were repulsed. Two days later Burnside's army retreated across the river and the campaign ended. (Library of Congress)

60. Chapter 12:   "The Pet Lamb and the Black Sheep; or, the Unhappy Shepherd." *Frank Leslie's Budget of Fun,* 1862. (Civil War Cartoon Collection, American Antiquarian Society)

61. Chapter 12:   "Butler Hanged-The Negro Freed-On Paper-1863." *Frank Leslie's Budget of Fun,* February 1, 1863. (Civil War Cartoon Collection, American Antiquarian Society)

62. Chapter 12:   "Monkey   Uncommon   Up,   Massa!" *Punch,* December 1, 1860.

63. Chapter 12:   Civil War Recruiting Poster: "Rally! Rally! Rally! To Men of Color!" (Courtesy of New-York Historical Society)

64. Chapter 12:   Unknown Union Soldier. (Library of Congress)

65. Chapter 13:   Lee in uniform. Julian Vannerson's photograph of Robert E. Lee in March 1864. Public Domain.

66. Chapter 13:   "Slaves working in The Cotton Fields." (Library of Congress)

67. Chapter 13:   "Digging Williams' Canal – 1862." In the summer of 1862, as ships of the West Gulf Blockading Squadron under Flag Officer David Glasgow Farragut bombarded the Vicksburg river defenses, a 3,000-man infantry brigade commanded by Brig. Gen. Thomas Williams, began work on a navigation channel that would bypass the Confederate batteries at Vicksburg. It was even believed by some that the man-made channel would possibly catch enough of the current's force to cause the river to change course, leaving the city high and dry, making Vicksburg militarily worthless without firing a shot. (National Park Service, Vicksburg National Military Park)

68. Chapter 13:   On April 1, 1863 women met at Belvidere Hill Baptist Church to demand food from Gov. John Letcher. If he didn't deliver, they would take it by force. They carried axes, hatchets, pistols, clubs, bayonets and knives. An illustration published in May 1863, *Harper's Weekly.* (Library of Congress)

69. Chapter 13:   "Sherman's men destroying railroad." Photo by G.N. Barnard, four men with crowbars twisting a rail, following Sherman's orders.. (Library of Congress)

70. Chapter 13:   "The Battles At Chancellorsville—Couch's Corps Forming Line Of Battle To Cover The Retreat Of The 11th Corps, 2d May, 1863." The flank attack was the pivotal moment in a massive battle that dramatically altered the course of the Civil War. *Harper's Weekly,* May 23, 1863. (Library of Congress)

71. Chapter 13:   Describing the sight of Lee amongst his cheering men after the battle, one observer wrote that "it must have been from some such scene that men in ancient days ascended to the dignity of gods." (Library of Congress)

72. Chapter 13:   Thomas J. "Stonewall" Jackson in a photograph dated by historians to April 1863, only a few weeks before the Battle of Chancellorsville. Jackson was on a reconnaissance expedition at approximately 9 p.m. when a Confederate officer on the left wing of the 18th North Carolina regiment spotted them through the trees by the moonlight, and, mistaking the group for Union cavalry, ordered his men to open fire. Jackson was wounded by three bullets—two in his left arm and one striking his right wrist. Upon hearing of the wounds that forced the amputation of Jackson's arm, Lee lamented,

"He has lost his left arm; but I have lost my right arm." (From the collection of Donald Olson)

73. Chapter 14:   "Burning of Jackson, Mississippi." After suffering two Union occupations, Jackson earned the nickname "Chimneyville" because of the number of chimneys left standing. Even Sherman, who established his headquarters in the Governor's Mansion, observed that the city "with the destruction committed by ourselves in May last and by the enemy during this siege, is one mass of charred ruins." (Old Capitol Museum, Jackson, Mississippi)

74. Chapter 14:   Cartoon from a northern newspaper poking fun at Confederate President Jefferson Davis' proclamation of a 'Day of fasting, humiliation and prayer,' 27 March 1863, during the American Civil War. *Harper's Weekly,* June 1862. (The Granger Collection, New York)

75. Chapter 14:   Sketch of Union infantrymen in a trench during the siege of Vicksburg, Mississippi. *Harper's Weekly,* June 1863. (Library of Congress)

76. Chapter 14:   Chambersburg, Pennsylvania 1863. Sentries were placed at the doors of all the principal houses, and the town was cleared of all but the military passing. Some of the troops marched straight through the town, and bivouacked on the Carlisle road. Others turned off to the right and occupied the Gettysburg turnpike. *Harper's Weekly,* June 1863. (Library of Congress)

77. Chapter 14:   The Shirley family's home, shown during the siege, was inside Union lines at Vicksburg. Removed from the dangerously exposed house, family members found shelter in a cave. (Old Courthouse Museum, Vicksburg, Mississippi)

78. Chapter 14:   Sketch of sacking of Wrightsville and bombing of the Wrightsville-Columbia Bridge by Maj. Gen. Jubal Early. Completed in 1834, the 5,620-foot-long Wrightsville-Columbia Bridge was the world's longest covered bridge. It featured 27 wooden spans, each 200 feet long, 40 feet wide, and stout enough to bear loaded train cars. It rose on stone pylons 15 feet above the high water mark. As an intersection of road, rail, river, and canal traffic, Wrightsville was of much greater strategic import to the invading Confederates than Gettysburg. When the powder smoke cleared,

one observer said, it could be seen that the explosion had "simply splintered the arch. It scarcely shook the bridge." *Harper's Weekly*, July 1863. (Library of Congress)

79.   Chapter 15:   Victory was long in coming at Vicksburg, but was crucial to the Union's success.   Illustration of celebration at Vicksburg capitol with U.S. Flag.   *Frank Leslie's Illustrated Newspaper*, July 1863. (Library of Congress)

80.   Chapter 15:   "BY TELEGRAPH. VICTORY!" The *North American and United States Gazette* announce the twin victories for the Union Army at Gettysburg and Vicksburg. Philadelphia, PA, July 8, 1863.

81.   Chapter 15:   Interview between Grant and Pemberton.   Print shows Union General Ulysses S. Grant and Confederate General John C. Pemberton discussing the terms of the capitulation of Vicksburg, bringing to an end the Union siege of the city.   Illus. in: Harper's pictorial history of the Civil War / Alfred H. Guernsey and Henry M. Alden. Chicago: The Puritan Press Co., c1894, v. 2, p. 478. (Library of Congress)

82.   Chapter 15:   "Battle of Gettysburg. Charge of Pickett's brigade on Cemetery Hill, Thursday night, July 2d, 1863." Wood engraving after a drawing, made on the battlefield, by A. Berghaus.   *Frank Leslies' Illustrated Newspaper.* (Library of Congress)

83.   Chapter 15:   "Confederate Column Retreating After Battle of Gettysburg." General Robert E. Lee ordered his Confederate army to retreat back to Virginia after their defeat in the bloody 3-day fight at Gettysburg, Pennsylvania.   It is said that his wagon train, carrying supplies and wounded soldiers, was 17-miles long.   The drawing shows one small portion of that wagon train. (Library of Congress)

84.   Chapter 15:   The dead at Gettysburg.   Photo by Timothy H. O'Sullivan. (National Archives)

85.   Chapter 15:   Photographer Alexander Gardner titled this "Unfit for Service – on the battlefield of Gettysburg. July 1863." This view shows a dead mule by a limber. Although it is a well-known picture from Gettysburg, where it was taken and to what military unit the mule and limber belonged is unknown. (Library of Congress)

86. Chapter 15: "Dead Confederate soldiers." Photographed by Alexander Gardner. (Library of Congress)

87. Chapter 15: President Abraham Lincoln. Dedication of the National Cemetery at Gettysburg, November 19, 1863. The only known image of Abraham Lincoln at Gettysburg was uncovered in 1952 at the National Archives. Photographed by Matthew Brady. (Library of Congress)

88. Chapter 16: Cartoon of President Abraham Lincoln sparring with Confederate President Jefferson Davis, circa 1861.

89. Chapter 16: Provost Guard of the 107th Colored Infantry, Fort Corcoran, Washington, D.C., 1863. (Library of Congress)

90. Chapter 16: Recruitment poster for the Massachusetts 54th Regiment, the first regiment to enlist Black men as soldiers for the Union Army during the Civil War. (J. E. Farwell & Co., 1863. Boston, MA)

91. Chapter 16: Alexander Stephens, Ga. Vice-President, CSA, between circa 1860 and circa 1865. As the war continued and the fortunes of the Confederacy sank lower, Stephens became more outspoken in his opposition to the Davis administration. Until the end of the war, he continued to press for actions aimed at bringing about peace. Brady National Photographic Art Gallery, Washington, D.C. (Library of Congress)

92. Chapter 16: Unidentified Confederate Soldier.

93. Chapter 17: Matthew Brady photograph of General Ulysses S. Grant. Grant was the son of Jesse Root Grant, a tanner, and Hannah Simpson, and he grew up in Georgetown, Ohio. Ulysses performed his share of chores on farmland owned by his father and developed considerable skill in handling horses. In 1839 Jesse secured for Ulysses an appointment to the United States Military Academy at West Point, New York, and pressured him to attend. Grant reversed his given names and enrolled as Ulysses Hiram; however, his congressional appointment was erroneously made in the name Ulysses S. Grant, the name he eventually accepted, maintaining that the middle initial stood for nothing. His classmates called him Sam. Grant ranked 21st in a class of 39 when he graduated from West Point in 1843, but he had distinguished himself in horsemanship and

showed considerable ability in mathematics. Upon graduation Grant was assigned as a brevet second lieutenant to the 4th U.S. Infantry, stationed near St. Louis, Missouri, where he fell in love with and married Julia Boggs Dent, the sister of his roommate at West Point. (Library of Congress)

94.　Chapter 17:　Ulysses S. Grant on Lookout Mountain, 1863. Grant is in the lower left corner. (National Archives)

95.　Chapter 17:　"Reception for U.S. Grant in the East Room of the White House, March 8, 1864." U.S. Grant arrived in Washington DC where he attended a reception that evening at the White House in his dusty campaign uniform unaware that it was a formal affair. Grant officially received his commission on March 9th assuming command of all the Union armies. (Library of Congress)

96.　Chapter 17:　"The war in Tennessee: Confederate massacre of black Union troops after the surrender at Fort Pillow, April 12, 1864." *Frank Leslie's Illustrated Newspaper*, May 7, 1864. (Library of Congress)

97.　Chapter 17:　Portrait of an unidentified Union soldier. (National Archives)

98.　Chapter 17:　A burial party inters the dead from the Battle of Gaines' Mill on the battlefield. (Library of Congress)

99.　Chapter 17:　Body of a Confederate soldier near Mrs. Alsop's house. Spotsylvania Court House, Va., vicinity. Photographed by Timothy Sullivan, May 24, 1864. (Library of Congress)

100.　Chapter 17:　Wounded from the Battle of the Wilderness, Fredericksburg, Virginia. Photographed by James Gardner. (Library of Congress)

101.　Chapter 17:　Meeting of Horace Greeley and Jeff Davis at Richmond published in *Harper's Weekly* July 1864. (Library of Congress)

102.　Chapter 17:　Union General William T. Sherman on Sam at Federal Fort No 7, Atlanta, Georgia, 1864. Photograph of the War in the West. After three and a half months of incessant maneuvering and much hard fighting, Sherman forced Hood to abandon the munitions center of the Confederacy. Sherman remained there, resting his war-worn men and accumulating supplies, for nearly two and a half months. During the occupation, George N. Barnard, official photographer of the Chief Engineer's Office, made the best documentary record of the war in the West; but much of what he photographed was destroyed in the fire that spread from the military facilities blown up at Sherman's departure on November 15. (Library of Congress)

103. Chapter 18:   Bank of Chambersburg & Franklin House, Chambersburg, Franklin Co., Pa., destroyed by the rebels under General John McCausland, July 30th, 1864. Photo shows buildings burned by the Confederate cavalry troops in Chambersburg, Pennsylvania, in reprisal for destruction by Union troops in the Shenandoah Valley. (Library of Congress)

104. Chapter 18:   Fighting in the Crater at Petersburg. (City of Petersburg, VA)

105. Chapter 18:   On July 30, 1864 Private Louis Martin of Co. E, 29th U.S. Colored Infantry took part in the battle of the Crater. His discharge form reads as follows: "Loss of right-arm and left-leg by amputation for shell and gunshot wounds received in battle at Petersburg on July 30, 1864 in charging the enemies works. In consequence of which is totally disabled for military service and civil occupation wholly." December 2, 1865. (National Archives)

106. Chapter 18:   "Lincoln/Ruin / M'Clellan/Peace". Democratic Party broadside, 1864. Following the Union victories at Vicksburg and Gettysburg, the Confederacy continued to fight on, in the hope that Lincoln would lose the 1864 election. Lincoln's popularity waned as the magnitude and swiftness of casualties from Grant's pursuit of Lee in Virginia stunned even the most ardent Union supporters. "The dissatisfaction with Mr. Lincoln grows to abhorrence," an opponent wrote. A few hundred Republicans, including abolitionist Frederick Douglass and suffragist Elizabeth Cady Stanton, formed the Radical Democracy party and nominated General John C. Frémont. It was Frémont who had freed slaves owned by Missouri rebels in 1861 only to be overturned by Lincoln. The Democrats, who mercilessly lambasted the military draft and emancipation of the slaves, called for a settlement with the Confederacy. "After four years of failure to restore the Union by the experiment of war," the platform stated,

"justice, humanity, liberty and the public welfare demand that immediate efforts be made for a cessation of hostilities." "I am going to be beaten ... and unless some great change takes place, badly beaten," said Lincoln. (The University of Chicago Library, Lincoln Collection)

107. Chapter 19:   "ATLANTA. Fall of the Rebel Stronghold." *New York Times*, September 3, 1864.

108. Chapter 19:   Period sketch of Union cavalry burning the Shenandoah Valley in the fall of 1864. (National Park Service)

109. Chapter 19:   View of Woodstock, sketched from the hill west of the Manassas Gap RR. Sheridan told his soldiers to destroy all of the wheat and hay and "seize all mules, horses, and cattle that may be useful" to the army. The soldiers were ordered to make the Shenandoah Valley "untenable for the raiding parties of the rebel army." Anything that the Union could use they would take, but everything else was to be destroyed. (From the James E. Taylor Sketchbook. c1864)

110. Chapter 19:   1862 Confederate Paper Money, $100 Bill from Richmond, Virginia.

111. Chapter 19:   Unidentified young soldier in Confederate infantry uniform, possibly a drummer boy. (Library of Congress)

112. Chapter 20:   "Lincoln wins his second Presidential election." *The New York Herald*, November 9, 1864. (Library of Congress)

113. Chapter 20:   "Letter from Abraham Lincoln to his Cabinet Members, August 23, 1864." (Abraham Lincoln Papers, Manuscript Division, Library of Congress)

114. Chapter 20:   Portrait photo of President Abraham Lincoln, taken on Nov. 8, 1863 by Alexander Gardner, 11 days before he delivered his Gettysburg Address. This is often referenced as the only photograph of Lincoln looking straight into the camera. (Library of Congress)

115. Chapter 20:   "Doctor Lincoln's New Elixir of Life" by Thomas Nast. *New York Illustrated News*, April 12, 1862, 368. (Courtesy of the New York State Library)

116. Chapter 21:   Telegram from General William T. Sherman to President Abraham Lincoln announcing the surrender of Savannah, Georgia, as a Christmas present to the President, December 22, 1864. "I beg to present you as a Christmas gift the city of Savannah with 150 heavy guns and plenty of ammunition and also about 25,000 bales of cotton," Sherman wrote. The brief message came as a huge relief to Lincoln, who had been out of touch with Sherman for several weeks, since the major general had embarked from Atlanta on his March to the Sea. In a reply to the telegram that's dated December 26, 1864, Lincoln wrote: "Many, many thanks for your Christmas gift." Although Savannah surrendered relatively easily, the March to the Sea, with its psychological tactics designed to undercut civilian support for the Confederacy, lives in Southern memory as one of the cruelest campaigns of the Civil War. (National Archives)

117. Chapter 21:   An 1868 engraving by Alexander Hay Ritchie depicting the March to the Sea. (Library of Congress)

118. Chapter 21:   A dead Confederate soldier as he lay in the trenches of Fort Mohone, 1865. Photograph by Thomas C. Roche. (Library of Congress)

119. Chapter 21:   "The U.S. House of Representatives celebrates the ratification of the 13th amendment abolishing slavery." After the House had failed to follow the Senate in mustering the two-thirds majority necessary to amend the Constitution the previous June, Representative James Ashley of Ohio revived the amendment. He noted that "the genius of history with iron pen is waiting to record our verdict...which shall declare America is free." The 119 to 56 vote sealed the victory for abolitionists' long battle against the "peculiar institution". Despite rules dictating decorum in the House Chamber, the roll call vote instigated jubilant celebration. The requisite three-quarters of the states ratified the amendment with the state of Georgia's approval on December 6, 1865. *Harper's Weekly*, 18 February 1865. (Library of Congress)

120. Chapter 21:   "The Peace Commission - Flying to Abraham's Bosom." The Hampton Roads Peace Conference aboard the USS River Queen, a Union transport ship, was arranged by Lincoln's adviser Francis P Blair Sr. Lincoln and his Secretary of State William H Seward met with Confederate representatives Vice President Alexander Hamilton Stephens, Assistant Secretary of War John A.

Campbell and Senator Robert M T Hunter. *Harper's Weekly*, February, 1865. (Library of Congress)

121. Chapter 21: "General Sherman's Entry into Columbia, South Carolina, February 17, 1865." *Harper's Weekly*, April 1, 1865. (Library of Congress)

122. Chapter 22: "Crowd at Lincoln's second inauguration, March 4, 1865." Photo shows a large crowd of people waiting during President Abraham Lincoln's inauguration, which was held on a rainy day at the U.S. Capitol grounds in Washington, D.C. In the background are Congressional boarding houses on A Street, N.E., between Delaware Ave. and First Street, N.E. (Library of Congress)

123. Chapter 22: Thousands of spectators stood in thick mud to hear Abraham Lincoln deliver his Second Inaugural Address from the East Portico of the Capitol Building on March 4, 1865. This photograph is the most famous photograph of the event. Lincoln stands in the center, with papers in his hand. According to White's *The Eloquent President*, John Wilkes Booth is visible in the photograph, in the top row right of center. (Library of Congress)

124. Chapter 22: "The Auction Sale." From *Uncle Tom's Cabin*, Volume I, facing page 174 by Harriet Beecher Stowe. Uncle Tom's Cabin was first published March 20, 1852. It was not the first anti-slavery novel, but it was by far the most successful. In the first year over 300,000 copies of her book were sold. In 1856, over two million copies were sold. Her book was translated into 13 different languages. When President Lincoln first met her he said, "So you're the little lady that started this big war."

125. Chapter 22: "With Malice Toward None...." Autograph book, ca. 1865. In a letter to Thurlow Weed written shortly after delivering his Second Inaugural Address, Lincoln wrote: "I expect the latter [the inaugural address] to wear as well as—perhaps better than—anything I have produced; but I believe it is not immediately popular." Lincoln reprised the closing paragraph of his address in this autograph book belonging to Caroline R. Wright, wife of former Indiana Governor Joseph Albert Wright. On loan from the Benjamin Shapell Family Manuscript Foundation. (Library of Congress)

126. Chapter 22: Frederick Douglass. Douglass escaped from slavery in 1838 after a harsh life of servitude in Maryland. He was later hired by William Lloyd Garrison as a speaker for the Anti-Slavery Society. He founded and edited the North Star, an abolitionist newspaper. President Ulysses S. Grant appointed Frederick Douglass Marshal of District of Columbia and Minister to Haiti; the highest appointed positions in the federal government to which a black American was appointed in the 19th Century. (National Portrait Gallery, Smithsonian Institution)

127. Chapter 23: "General Sheridan at the Battle of Five Forks, April 1, 1865." Major General Philip H. Sheridan assumed command of the Army of the Shenandoah in late August of 1864. The bulk of his army consisted of what was the Cavalry Corps of the Army of the Potomac. Sheridan drove Jubal Early's Confederates out of the valley, destroying much of the useable war materials in the area. Sheridan's mobile strike force arrived in Petersburg in late March and Grant immediately put them to work against Lee. *Harper's Weekly*, April 22, 1865. (Library of Congress)

128. Chapter 23: "Citizens of the State, People of Richmond" poster. When Grant was appointed general-in-chief of Union armies after Gettysburg, he determined to follow Lincoln's directions to target Robert E. Lee and the Army of Northern Virginia and not the Confederate capital. Yet Richmond necessarily loomed large because Lee determined to defend it: it was his logistical lifeline. The Overland Campaign of 1864 was launched in the Wilderness and quickly became a slugfest in the woods. Lee inflicted horrific casualties, but Grant relentlessly continued his attack. By June, the campaign had settled into a siege at Richmond's backdoor—the city of Petersburg. As Lee and many Confederates knew, it was only a matter of time before he must abandon the capital or be encircled by the Union juggernaut. As the Confederate lines grew thinner and thinner during the nine-and-a-half-month siege, people in Richmond faced the real possibility of starvation. On March 25, 1865, Lee tried to break through Grant's lines, only to be repulsed. Just days later, Grant launched an all-out assault on Lee's army. Lee was forced to notify President Davis on April 2, 1865, that Richmond had to be evacuated.

129. Chapter 23: "Richmond, Virginia, after Its Conquest. The City of Richmond, from the James River." After evacuating Confederate

forces destroyed bridges across the James River in April, 1865, occupying Federal troops built pontoon bridges as temporary replacements. (*Illustrated London News*, May 20, 1865)

130. Chapter 23: "The Union Army Entering Richmond, VA., April 3," from *Frank Leslie's Illustrated Newspaper*, April 25, 1865. (Library of Congress)

131. Chapter 23: "Abraham Lincoln and Emancipated Slaves, April 1865." Richmond fell on April 3, 1865, and President Lincoln went to the fallen city the very next day. Throngs of slaves were in the streets, celebrating their first day of freedom, and welcoming Lincoln. Thomas Nast captured this historic event. Lincoln did, if only briefly, get to see the fruit of his leadership and resolve. He was able to see the grateful tears of the emancipated, and hear their cheers of appreciation. Nast wasn't present for the April 4 event but made the engraving based on eyewitness accounts. *Harper's Weekly*, February 24, 1866. (Library of Congress)

132. Chapter 23: "President Lincoln visiting the late residence of Jefferson Davis in Richmond, Va." On April 4, 1865, Abraham Lincoln visited Richmond, Virginia. Greeted by a throng of citizens, including many former slaves enjoying their freedom, Lincoln made his way to the Confederate White House, where he sat down in a chair he believed must have been used by Jefferson Davis and spoke to people while in Davis's library. From *Frank Leslie's Illustrated Newspaper*, April 29, 1865. (Library of Congress)

133. Chapter 23: "Ruins of the Arsenal, Richmond, Virginia, April 1865." Soldiers standing in the ruins of an arsenal in Richmond, Va., with cannon balls stacked in the courtyard. During the evacuation of Richmond, President Jefferson Davis ordered that all buildings and bridges should be set on fire to prevent the Union army from getting through the city. Alexander Gardner, Albumen print. (Museum Purchase, Lloyd O. and Marjorie Strong Coulter Fund.)

134. Chapter 23: Poster announcing the Surrender of General Lee on April 9, 1865.

135. Chapter 23: "Palm Sunday," by Thomas Nast. Poster announcing the surrender of General Lee at the Appomattox courthouse in Virginia ending the Civil War on April 9, 1865. It was

Palm Sunday when Confederate General Robert E. Lee surrendered to Union General Ulysses S. Grant in the front parlor of the Wilmar McLean home at Appomattox Court House, Virginia, effectively bringing the bloodiest war in American history toward conclusion. *Harper's Weekly*, May 20, 1865. (Library of Congress)

136. Chapter 23:   Union soldiers pose in April 1865 in front of Appomattox Courthouse. Photographed by Timothy H. O'Sullivan, April 1865. (Library of Congress)

137. Chapter 23:   Ely Parker, or Donehogawa, Seneca chief, military secretary to U. S. Grant and Commissioner of Indian Affairs. Ely S. Parker, Civil War General and Seneca Chief, was born on the reservation near Indian Falls, New York in 1828. Prior to the war, he studied Law and Engineering. Harvard would not admit him because of his race. The New York Bar would not consider his application since he wasn't an American citizen. Ely turned his attention to Civil Engineering. He worked on the Genesee Valley Canal and, in 1849, the Erie Canal. Parker received an appointment by the Treasury Department in 1857, which took him to Galena, Illinois as superintendent of Construction on two government buildings. It was in Galena that he made the acquaintance of Ulysses S. Grant with whom Parker developed a lifelong friendship. With the outbreak of the Civil War, Ely S. Parker offered to raise a regiment of Iroquois Volunteers, but the New York Governor refused. Next Parker offered his services to the Army's Chief of Engineers and was again turned down. In 1863, with Grant's endorsement, the Army finally accepted Parker as a Captain of Engineers. In 1864, Parker was promoted to lieutenant-colonel and became Grant's military secretary. Lieutenant-Colonel Parker campaigned with Grant against Robert E. Lee until Appomattox. In 1867, he was promoted to the rank of Brigadier General in the Regular Army. Photographed around 1867. (Smithsonian Institution)

138. Chapter 23:   High Bridge over the Appomattox, near Farmville, Va., April 1865. Photographed by Timothy H. O'Sullivan. (Library of Congress)

139. Eulogy: Lady Liberty (Columbia) weeping over Lincoln's body, by Thomas Nast. *Harper's Weekly*, April 29, 1865. (Library of Congress)

140. <u>Eulogy:</u>   Abraham Lincoln. Photo by Alexander Gardner taken at Gardner's Gallery in Washington, DC, on Sunday, February 5, 1865. This last photo in Lincoln's last photo session from life was long thought to have been made on April 10, 1865, but more recent research has indicated the earlier date in February. Image shows crack in original negative, which was broken and discarded back in 1865. The original surviving print is at the National Portrait Gallery. (Library of Congress)

Made in the USA
Middletown, DE
11 December 2020